FIELDS OF PLAY IN
MODERN DRAMA

THOMAS R. WHITAKER

Fields of Play in
Modern Drama

PRINCETON UNIVERSITY PRESS

Copyright © 1977 by Princeton University Press
Published by Princeton University Press,
Princeton, New Jersey
In the United Kingdom:
Princeton University Press, Guildford, Surrey

ALL RIGHTS RESERVED

Library of Congress Cataloging in Publication Data
will be found on the last printed page of this book

Published with the aid of The Paul Mellon Fund
at Princeton University Press

This book has been composed in
Linotype Times Roman

Printed in the United States of America
by Princeton University Press,
Princeton, New Jersey

—remembering a player,

BARTON CLARK RIPPY
1924–1948

CONTENTS

ARJUNA: And now, Krishna, I wish to learn about the Field and the Knower of the Field. . . .

KRISHNA: This body is called the Field. . . . Recognize me to be in all Fields the Knower of the Field . . . also called the Witness. . . . As the one sun illuminates the whole world, so the Dweller in the Field illuminates the whole Field.

—Bhagavad-Gita

SOUL: You say "act"? My soul thirsts for action. In this miserable part where would there be room for a single act?

ANGEL: Play the part, and its meaning will be revealed to you.

—The Salzburg Great Theatre
of the World

FIELDS OF PLAY IN
MODERN DRAMA

A RETROSPECTIVE
WORD

THIS RATHER informal essay is the meditation of an amateur who has risked getting lost in the theater. On coming back with what may seem an unusual kind of dramatic criticism and a sketch for the reinterpretation of modern drama (in terms of the power of all drama to lead us beyond the histrionic and objectifying self toward participation in the intersubjective consciousness that grounds our play), I have searched for guideposts that might make the journey less puzzling for the reader. Perhaps none would be more helpful than the two snatches of dialogue that I have now placed as epigraphs. In the *Bhagavad-Gita* the warrior who shuns his proper field of action must learn from the avatar of all witnessing to see the inaction that is in action, the action that is in inaction. But in *The Salzburg Great Theatre of the World* the modern soul who thirsts for action can receive from the witnessing angel no such traditional teaching: he must more or less blindly play his part in order to learn its meaning—and will find himself at the moment of crisis a beggar whose single true action will seem to be inaction. Neither of these situations can make very much sense to us if we haven't already begun to perceive within our own fields the dialogical reciprocity of all acting and witnessing. And the line of action in Hofmannsthal's play (or in this essay) will strike us as appropriate only if our modern sense of the problematic nature of existence allows for something like the faith that Theodore Roethke has expressed in "The Waking": "I learn by going where I have to go." Can "playing" be understood as at least one of our proper fields of action? Can our fragmented modern theater be understood as providing self-illuminating fields of play that point us toward their common ground? If so, perhaps we could even imagine a modern and western branch of the path of action within which this essay might more or less blindly play its part.

My extensive debts to the professionals—in the theater and out—would be very hard to summarize. I have placed at the end a listing of some of the texts behind this text. Here let me simply express my gratitude to the many persons—actors, directors, scholars, students, friends—from whom I have learned something about the perplexing life of drama. Perhaps my most long-standing debt is suggested in the dedication: to the memory of one who for a brief time shared some attempts at script-writing, acting, and directing, and who managed to teach me more than I was ready to understand about the playfulness of life. And my most recent debt is to three perspicacious readers of the manuscript—Ruby Cohn, Michael Goldman, and Jerry Sherwood—whose bracing combination of skepticism and good will has made the process of revision an unusual pleasure.

I am also grateful to the University of Iowa for an Old Gold Summer Fellowship and to the Danforth Foundation for an E. Harris Harbison Award, both of which assisted the writing of this essay. Occasions for trying out some of its formulations have been generously provided by the University of Iowa, Michigan State University, Bowling Green State University, the University of Pittsburgh, Oberlin College, and Yale University. Much of the argument of chapter 4 appeared in very different form in *Papers in Dramatic Theory and Criticism*, ed., David Knauf (Iowa City: University of Iowa Press, 1969). Most of chapter 2 appeared in *Centennial Review*, 16 (Winter 1972). I thank the editor and the publisher for permission to reprint.

Finally, I must thank certain publishers who have given permission for rather extensive quotations: Grove Press, Inc., for quotations from *Happy Days*, by Samuel Beckett (copyright © 1961 by Grove Press, Inc.); Random House, Inc., for quotations from *The Caucasian Chalk Circle*, by Bertolt Brecht with Ruth Berlau (translated by Ralph Manheim in *Collected Plays*, Volume 7, copyright © 1974 by Stefan S. Brecht); and Harcourt Brace Jovanovich, Inc., for quotations from *Murder in the Cathedral*, by T. S. Eliot (copyright © 1963 by T. S. Eliot).

ONE

SPEAKING OF PLAYING

I WANT TO speak here of the playing that is implied by some important modern scripts, and I must begin by confessing agreement with two rather bold convictions. One has been voiced by Don Quixote: "Nothing, in fact, more truly portrays us as we are and as we would be than the play and the players." And the other by Schiller: "Man plays only when he is in the full sense of the word a man, and *he is only wholly Man when he is playing.*" But what can such convictions mean today? What *is* this playing that calls itself Man?

Perhaps modern drama has been most centrally a posing of just that question. And the answer at which it often seems to have arrived is rather unsettling: Playing is the mask of nothing at all. In the nineteenth century, of course, Hazlitt could praise Shakespeare by saying, "He is nothing in himself." And a few decades later Bernard Shaw, the self-declared rival of that supreme actor-playwright, could say with characteristic modesty, "I understand everything and everyone and I am nothing and no one." But the distinctively modern nuance may become audible in such pronouncements only when they have been quoted by Jorge Luis Borges, or when that labyrinthine ironist begins a parable on Shakespeare with the quiet assertion: "There was no one in him. . . ."

Among modern writers Borges is far from alone in suspecting that the actor-playwright may perceive and live a truth against which most of us defend ourselves through willed ignorance. In Hugo von Hofmannsthal's "Prologue to Brecht's *Baal*," an actor who is playing himself finds occasion to declare: "The actor is the amoeba among all living things and therefore he is the symbolic man." In the year of that prologue, 1926, Brecht himself wrote: "The notion of a continuous I is a myth. Man is a constantly disintegrating and self-renewing atom." And Pirandello, of course, had dramatized a good many permutations of exactly this predicament. Such instances point to what must become in this essay not only my theme but also my field of action. For I can speak of our problematic playing only from within the predicament it explores. Where else, in truth, could I—or any "I"—possibly be? Those who seem to stand outside the contemporary situation and write with objectivity about drama as a cultural phenomenon—well, what are they but rhetorical *personae*, players made up for the occasion? I prefer to admit the histrionic nature of any self-proclaimed "I"—and so acknowledge the seriousness of the plays in which I participate.

Participate? I who am neither "actor" nor "director" by profession? Of course. How could we ever begin to understand a play by remaining entirely outside it? And where would that "outside" be? A play is no external object. It does not "make a statement" about a human condition from which it has somehow withdrawn. Nor does it merely "imitate" an action. A play is a present action, a form of attentive playing, and its full meaning must therefore include the fact of our participation in it. We always participate through two mutually inclusive modes. When we act, we present ourselves to witnesses. When we witness, we attend to actors. But every actor is also an implicit witness, every witness an implicit actor. From such reciprocity, each moment in a play is shaped. The whole play is therefore the form of our shared acting and witnessing, a distinctive field of playing that we compose within the intersubjective field of play that makes it possible.

Perhaps we could easily enough begin to speak of certain forms of acting and witnessing that we have experienced in the theater—though I haven't seen this attempted in any sustained way. But should the criticism of drama be limited to accounts of actual performances? Scripts, like musical scores, are normative invitations. And though a major script leaves open a wide range of directorial choices and audience responses, it implies with some precision not only the "objectives" and "subtexts"

of the *dramatis personae* but also the lines of action and sequences of perception to be shared by the implied participants.
In doing so, it establishes a web of relations between the action
"imitated" or performed and our present action of performance
in the theater. Can these forms of playing be elucidated prior to
—or at least apart from—the specific choices, contingencies,
and experiences of an actual performance? And can "I" begin
to elucidate them without evading the ways in which they call
into question any identity that "I" may assume?

Dramatic criticism of the usual kind may not be quite suited
to this task. Despite any liveliness of "personal" style, it posits a
critic who is a fixed identity and a play that is external to the
critic and to everyone else. But what is the alternative? Without
presuming to know the answer, I want to risk here what might
turn out to be a suitably playful procedure. I propose that we
move through a sequence of notes, commentaries, dialogues, and
fictions that will allow speech to proceed from a locus that can
shift, multiply, or dissolve in response to some of the challenges
offered by various plays. We might well begin with some notes
on the reflexive theatricality that now dominates our stage. Perhaps we could reach some hypotheses as to how the major
plays of our time have focused our predicament as players. In
later chapters we might test those hypotheses against ten or
twelve plays from Ibsen to the present. But any testing of
hypotheses (as Michael Polanyi has noted) is a double process:
as we learn about the field into which we are inquiring, we
simultaneously unfold the implications of the definitions and
assumptions that underlie our inquiry. Perhaps, then, our double
process of interrogating some major plays and disclosing the
implications of "our shared acting and witnessing" can lead
toward some reinterpretation of modern drama. We might even
find that the most problematic of modern scripts tacitly recognize playing to be not just the futile activity of a histrionic self
or the mask of an empty nothing but a manifestation of that nothing or Act to which we may open ourselves when ceasing to
claim an objectified identity.

In sketching this possible movement, I must say "we" because several voices will no doubt ask to be heard within "me"

—and because you who read are necessarily speaking these lines, too. If I can't be single, we are not irreducibly double— and happily enough, "for a *We* seems to me finer," as Hofmannsthal wrote to Martin Buber in December of 1926, "than this doubtful *I*." Such dialogical puzzles must already complicate any talk of testing hypotheses because they are among the conditions of all talk, as of all play. Language itself is a participatory act. Even when mediated by print, our meanings inhabit a field that cannot finally be reduced to a collection of determinate objects. Indeed, Maurice Merleau-Ponty has argued that the "order of instructive spontaneity," which is "inaccessible to psychologism and historicism no less than to dogmatic metaphysics," is best revealed to us by the phenomenology of speech:

> When I speak or understand, I experience that presence of others in myself or of myself in others which is the stumbling-block of the theory of intersubjectivity. I experience that presence of what is represented which is the stumbling-block of the theory of time, and I finally understand what is meant by Husserl's enigmatic statement, "Transcendental subjectivity is intersubjectivity." To the extent that what I say has meaning, I am a different "other" for myself when I am speaking; and to the extent that I understand, I no longer know who is speaking and who is listening.

Such puzzles may also warn us that speakers who enter the "order of instructive spontaneity" or the fields of play had better not try to predict their own future in great detail. In *The Notebooks of Malte Laurids Brigge*, Rilke's alter-ego has written: "Let us be honest about it, then; we have no theatre, any more than we have a God: for this, community is needed." In the hope of undermining such a temptingly desperate conclusion, I propose a way of inquiry into our shared acting-and-witnessing. But if "I" propose, who disposes? And if "you" resist being included in what may seem a rather free-wheeling "we"? In our moments of doubt, let that Salzburg Angel remind us: "Play the part. . . ."

TWO

PLAYING THE PLAYER

Is IT POSSIBLE that modern drama, which has been so plural, such a tricky shape-shifter, has a central direction and meaning? Let these notes at least play with a hunch.

PERHAPS we know today what Hamlet meant to tell the Player. The purpose of playing, both at the first and now, was and is to hold the mirror up to playing. For what else can "nature" mean? We find ourselves playing. Reflecting on our condition, we begin to play the player.

Or so it must seem, more than a century after Peer Gynt first peeled his onion. Since then we've had mirrors of all shapes and sizes. In *Rosmersholm* and *Three Sisters* the fictions of realism probe the self-deceptive fictions that we are. In *Heartbreak House*, where Hector and Hesione play Get the Guests and Peel the Label many years before Albee's George and Martha heard of those games, a bolder rhetoric exposes our rhetorical masks. Such various mirrors-within-mirrors as *The Ghost Sonata, Six Characters in Search of an Author, The Caucasian Chalk Circle, The Balcony,* and *Waiting for Godot* all bring into focus our onion-skin identity. And many lesser plays—like Molnar's *Play's the Thing,* which affectionately burlesques what Shaw called Sardoodledom, or Shepard's *Tooth of Crime,* which pays such ambivalent tribute to the kingdom of rock— hold the mirror up to the commercial theater as an image of our off-stage theatricality. Indeed, what purpose other than that of playing the player has so completely informed the kaleidoscopic variety of our dramatic styles—from *The Importance of Being*

Earnest and *King Ubu* to *What the Butler Saw* and *The King Must Die*?

A striking number of modern plays and productions also owe their life to a decision to play *with* an earlier script. At one extreme is Brecht's *Roundheads and the Peakheads,* which sustains our interest today primarily as an ingenious response to *Measure for Measure.* As we witness the translation of one ethos into another, we hear Brecht's dry pronouncement: ". . . *wir können Shakespeare ändern, wenn wir ihn ändern können.*" Remake the master if you're man enough! And even Bernard Sobel's politically committed production in 1973 for the Ensemble Théâtral de Gennevilliers couldn't resist bringing the Viceroy on stage at the end in Elizabethan costume. At the other extreme are such collages as Charles Marowitz's *Hamlet* or Tadashi Suzuki's *On the Dramatic Passions II.* Composed for the actress Kayako Shiraishi and the Waseda Shōgekijō, Suzuki's sequence of extracts from popular theater and fiction is an evocation and exorcism of the demonic life of the collective imagination and a brilliant "re-reading" of Kabuki style. And the broad middle range of such playing with plays—adaptation, confrontation, sardonic commentary, or wry burlesque—may be suggested by Hofmannsthal's *Tower,* Grotowski's *Constant Prince,* Dürrenmatt's *Play Strindberg,* Ionesco's *Macbett,* and Stoppard's *Travesties.*

Directors today can hardly resist adding further histrionic perspectives to plays that in themselves may be complex studies of role-playing—as in John Barton's *Troilus and Cressida* of 1968 and Peter Brook's *Midsummer Night's Dream* of 1971. The recent Molière tercentenary occasioned some no less symptomatic productions. Jean-Louis Barrault's *Bourgeois Gentilhomme* gradually overwhelmed the conservative elocutionary style of the sponsoring Comédie Française with the director's personal idiom of dionysiac celebration. In Jean-Louis Thamin's production of *L'Étourdi* at the Théâtre National of Strasbourg, the carnival-players within the play were transformed into players who *present* the play—and the stock figures of the main plot accordingly became their puppets. It's not surprising that in this American bicentennial year Alan Arkin should choose to revive Maxwell Anderson's *Joan of Lorraine*, with the rehearsal scenes updated by the cast's own improvisations. Anderson's play, as Arkin told a reporter, is really "about both Joan and the theater."

Even a social statement now seems to want chiefly to mirror histrionic behavior—as in Dürrenmatt's *Physicists*, Fugard's *Boesman and Lena*, Kopit's *Indians*, or Dorst's *Great Curse Before the City Walls*. Kenneth Brown has rather predictably moved from the routines of *The Brig* to those of *The Green Room*, a play that suggests Wilder's *Our Town* reincarnate in the Living Theatre, a community of actors who are always acting. It is almost inevitable that Ariane Mnouchkine's co-operative Théâtre du Soleil, when asking in 1971 and 1972 the meaning of the French Revolution, should find itself playing the *playing* of those historical events: first as carnival players who celebrate the recent events of *1789* and then as more naively histrionic citizens (living behind the self-conscious glitter of the prologue's operatic stage) who tell of their participation in the events of *1793*. And it's no accident that *Marchands de Ville*, a composition of 1972 by the Théâtre de l'Aquarium which attacks speculative urban renewal, should find its liveliest moments in scenes dominated by the wheeler-dealer Volcani and the triple-top-hatted and triple-frock-coated triumvirate of the Banque Talbin, who caricature the financial-governmental complex.

But if the stage now seems to want to be everywhere, perhaps that's because it already is. Environmental theater arises in a theatrical environment. Courses in acting use texts by Eric Berne on gamesmanship. *Viet Rock* improvised a question within the public relations script that was selling the destruction of Viet Nam. Is our entire culture an ominous god out of the machine? *America Hurrah.* "Life itself," Abbie Hoffman could shout as he ran into the streets on TV, "is theater!" But wouldn't our obsession astonish even that Richard II who so knowingly smashed his own mirror? Or that Perkin Warbeck who refused to let the scaffold itself frighten him out of his role as pretender? Aware that life is a question of playing, Hamlet now becomes a nameless man who condemns himself to play

Henry IV forever. Or else a Hamm who yawns to himself in a
bare shelter after the devastation of the world: "Me—to play."

∿∿∿∿∿∿∿∿∿∿

ALL RIGHT: let that stand as a first impression of where we are.
The modern theme, I suppose, is consciousness of consciousness.
As our late romanticism gives another twist to the baroque,
every point of view tends to include an insistence that it is
only a point of view. Every medium becomes its own most
important subject. We paint painting. We make poems about
poetry, fictions about fiction, films about film. And we play
the player.

But something is wrong with that formula. What *is* playing?
Is it pretending? deceiving? manipulating? imitating? exploring? performing? participating? frolicking? celebrating? Is it the
deliberate histrionic madness of Pirandello's nameless man who
plays Henry IV, or the world's more self-deceptive and murderous form of that madness? And what about the playing through
which we *discover* that nameless man? Is "playing the player"
just an irresponsible equivocation, a bit of fashionable fraudu-
lence? Or does the phrase point to an inescapable ambiguity?

∿∿∿∿∿∿∿∿∿∿

LET'S begin with the most obvious meaning of that phrase—one
that Shakespeare's Jaques and Macbeth understood well enough.
When playing expands to include everything, it can shrivel to
mean nothing. But what once could be the self-deluding
thought of a comic or tragic character now seems to become
the burden of entire plays. From Ibsen to Pirandello, Strindberg
to Genet, Chekhov to Beckett, dramatic styles themselves seem
bent on reducing life to inauthenticity and emptiness. Translated into more explicit and less demanding form, such histrionic nihilism now attains popular success.

"Give us this day our daily mask," says Guildenstern or
maybe Rosencrantz. Uncertain of their own names, the non-
protagonists of Tom Stoppard's *Rosencrantz & Guildenstern
Are Dead* might almost be Beckett's Vladimir and Estragon reincarnate in the debater's style of the Oxford Union. They have

been sent for—but why? What must they do? And to what end? They are two characters in search of an *explication de texte*, two muddled players in reluctant pursuit of the roles they already play. Frantic and inert by turns, they repeatedly digress into the self-parody of gamesmanship—tossing coins, spinning theories, playing lengthy sets of questions. They might easily say to themselves with Beckett's Clov: "you must be there better than that if you want them to let you go." But they would be wrong. Their world doesn't really demand their presence. That intense realm of authenticity with which they play hide-and-seek is itself nothing but theater. It is *Hamlet*, and it already contains them. Even *The Murder of Gonzago* here contains their doubles and enacts their death. A mousetrap, indeed. The Elizabethan convention of the play-within-the-play has become the infinite regression of plays-that-enclose-the-play. That's why Rosencrantz and Guildenstern must also seem our own clarified doubles, giving colloquial voice to our anxious inauthenticity within a closed theatrical world. Compared to them, we are—as so often in Pirandello's plays—a mere flux, a waste of forms, a sea of troubles. For the characters of *Waiting for Godot*, we are a bog. And here, when Hamlet comes down-stage and spits in the sea, we spit right back in his eye.

The world of *Rosencrantz & Guildenstern Are Dead* requires not their presence but their absence, not their authentic openness here and now but their resignation to the fatality of nonexistence. In *Waiting for Godot* the chance of any desired outcome is always fifty-fifty. But *Are Dead* is ruled by a design that makes every flip of the coin an ominous call for "heads" and turns the shell-games into a barrel-game in which Rosencrantz and Guildenstern and Hamlet and the Player become so many interchangeable peas. Just before being blacked out by a spotlight as ruthless as that which controls the action in Beckett's play called *Play*, Guildenstern or maybe Rosencrantz names his end: "It's the absence of presence, nothing more." Impelled by that final cause, these bumbling comedians speed as swiftly toward Absence as does Genet's more skillfully fake Bishop in *The Balcony*. Perhaps they might say with Beckett's Hamm

"Absent, always. It all happened without me." Life here is a dubious fiction, the mask of an incredible death. And Hamlet's eloquent question—"To be or not to be"—has become one of many dumb shows.

The *raisonneur* of this clever pastiche is of course the Player. Everyone else plays somewhat inadvertently or with intense absence of mind, but the Player knowingly plays himself. His troupe does "on stage the things that are supposed to happen off." But the stage is anywhere and the Player always in costume. Here is a man—no, a male part—who can say, "I *start* on." A connoisseur of our obscene strutting and fretting, he sells its open secret to any passer-by—and for eight guilders you can participate. But in these indifferent times, Genet's transvestite ritual has become a tired farce. When the Envoy in *The Balcony* elucidates the mystery of Absence, he describes the Queen as engrossed in "an infinite meditation." She is "moving rapidly towards immobility." She "is embroidering and . . . she is not embroidering. She picks her nose, examines the pickings and lies down again." But when Stoppard's Player rebukes his Player-Queen, he strips the embroidery from such infinitely absent refinement: "Stop picking your nose, Alfred. When Queens have to they do it by a cerebral process passed down in the blood."

Death too for this Player is no elaborate studio rite but just another competent routine: he resurrects himself with professional aplomb after being stabbed by a collapsible dagger. Is he then the eternal opposite of the annihilated Rosencrantz and Guildenstern? Not really. Old actors never die, and they feed the right questions to their straightmen: "Do you know what happens to old actors?" "What?" "Nothing. They're still acting." As the Player has earlier said, "the single assumption which makes our existence viable" is "that somebody is *watching*"— without which we're "stripped naked in the middle of nowhere and pouring ourselves down a bottomless well." Self-conscious life, for *Are Dead*, is playing the player, an elusive absence signifying nothing.

BUT can I believe that interpretation? No. Does the play ask
us to believe it? Not really. I've made the usual critical mistake.
A play's meaning isn't simply the statement it seems to make,
the action it performs, or the world it presents. What happens
when we attend *Rosencrantz & Guildenstern Are Dead* at the
Old Vic? We relax for an evening of flirting with the void. We
play with our anxieties, secure in the fiction that we are even
brighter than our brothers in motley. We pretend to believe in
nothing, morally confident that our innocent pastime elicits a
generous good humor toward our vexed alter-egos and an
amused indignation toward the tyrannical design that sweeps
them to their end. We can afford to be amused. After all,
whose is that tyranny? Stoppard's—and ours. We share buoy-
antly in the play's ruthless control of its action We have become Shakespeare. We have become Death. Lords of absence,
we *play* those players.

   Rosencrantz & Guildenstern Are Dead cancels itself very
neatly. If plays were statements, it would be a phony statement
that everything is phony. Stoppard has dramatized the paradox
of the Cretan liar, and with a studied triviality that might bring
a glint to the ghostly eye of Oscar Wilde. Does life signify
nothing? Life is art, and we are its impotent masters.

〰〰〰〰〰〰〰

BUT can I believe *that* interpretation? Not entirely. How could
such a self-deceptive aestheticism become absolute in the
theater? It pretends that characters and players are things in
an objective field, a space in which we manipulate and observe.
Its main paradox, a constantly hinted source of anxiety, is that
every human subject must then really be an object. Every
manipulator must really be an empty and passive spectacle for
another manipulator. But surely our enjoyment of that very
anxiety suggests that the paradox can't be final? More obviously and immediately than any other art, drama is an act of
man-with-man. A play always exists *among* us. It contains not
"characters" but roles-played-by-actors-for-us. The *dramatis
personae* are not people but the partial masks of the actors'

lives and ours while we participate in the performance. Why do we forget that when we start talking about a play's meaning?

A play is grounded not in impotent mastery but in spontaneous reciprocity, inherent mutuality. Our ordinary act of listening includes a virtual speaking: we "hear" another as he becomes a voice in our own continuing dialogue. And our ordinary act of watching includes a virtual gesture, to which we attune ourselves. A play focuses that reciprocity and reflects it further. For those who are discovering their roles, and for those who are responding to the actors' gestures of discovery, a play is a collaborative miming that is lifted moment by moment into the light of the attention. We are both "outside" and "inside" its action, in a double "now" that is a mimed present and a present miming. A play's meaning must therefore reside in its total form of acting-and-witnessing, even when the play pretends otherwise. Its "playing upon" is grounded in a "playing with." The empty space in which we manipulate and observe is an abstraction from this full and living space constituted by our mutuality. The objective field of play depends upon our intersubjective field of play.

That's why the National Theatre Company's production of *Rosencrantz & Guildenstern Are Dead* most belied itself when it was most lively. Moment by moment Guildenstern was seeking emptily, in relative isolation, through repeated misunderstandings, for a meaningless role that he was already doomed to play. But moment by moment Edward Petherbridge was exploring with freshness and precision, and in close rapport with his stage partners and with us, the meaning of being a Guildenstern. Petherbridge's clowning as a player-in-spite-of-himself was a graceful clumsiness, an alert befuddlement, a shared understanding of ignorance. And it wasn't at all like the Player's playing of himself *within* this play. Stoppard's Player is a self-conscious nothing who sardonically attains a fake existence by tempting others to watch his old tricks. But Petherbridge starts with us in a very different field of play, through which we move toward shared discoveries. Though the Player can be *raisonneur* for his own emptily histrionic world, he can't describe the playing that discloses his world to

us. He can't even explain how he can join Guildenstern on the
stage of the Old Vic as a delightfully melodramatic presence, a
fresh version of stale ham.

Does the play then fall apart? Not quite. What is its spine,
its more than Stanislavskian objective? To play the player. The
characters share that action in various ways, all limited by the
tyrannical design of histrionic nihilism. But actors and audience also share that action, and we play those players in ways
that combine a self-gratifying aestheticism and a lively reciprocity. A light spirit of paradox allows us to reconcile a so-
phistic denial and a tacit affirmation of our field of mutual
presence. But wouldn't *Rosencrantz & Guildenstern Are Dead*
be stronger and more richly coherent if it were yet more self-
aware—if it more fully recognized its equivocation? Then it
might probe some of the questions it provokes: How can we
play so many ways at once? And what leads us to refresh ourselves by exploring our nothingness?

SURELY some plays do probe those questions. What about
Beckett's *Happy Days*? Even emptier, more claustral, more
desolate than Stoppard's play, *Happy Days* is also more astrin-
gently tonic, more fully humane. Though it includes an apparent statement of impotence and absence, an enactment of
aesthetic mastery, and a celebration of our reciprocity, it resists any attempt to lay out those meanings in a neat dialectic.
It denies us the luxury of distinguishing the muddled clown
from the nihilistic *raisonneur*, or the theatrical artifact from
the participatory playing.

Our scene: an expanse of scorched grass, rising in the center
to a low mound where Winnie is buried up to the waist, fixed
there by some cosmic decree in the timeless time after the end
of all Endgames. (Does this parody of hell, in which a parasol
will soon burst into flame, represent our world?) When wakened
by an off-stage bell, she goes through what would be, in the
"old style," her daily routine. (Who rings that bell? Is our hell
a theater?) With a hesitant but inexhaustible flow of exclama-
tions, doubts, reversals, qualifications, and digressions, she

prattles on about her dwindling collection of objects (tooth-brush, mirror, comb and brush, parasol, revolver, music-box), runs through her repertoire of sentimental memories, and counts with relish her empty blessings. Now and then she gets a response from her lustful and sluggish Willie, who sun-bathes out of sight behind her mound. But mostly she seems to talk to herself—even when, plucking at the scorched grass, she addresses to Willie an account of her own loquacity:

> Not that I flatter myself you hear much, no Willie, God forbid. (*Pause.*) Days perhaps when you hear nothing. (*Pause.*) But days too when you answer. (*Pause.*) So that I may say at all times, even when you do not answer and perhaps hear nothing, Something of this is being heard, I am not merely talking to myself, that is in the wilderness, a thing I could never bear to do—for any length of time. (*Pause.*) That is what enables me to go on, go on talking that is. (*Pause.*) Whereas if you were to die—(*smile*)—to speak in the old style—(*smile off*)—or go away and leave me, then what would I do, what *could* I do, all day long, I mean between the bell for waking and the bell for sleep? (*Pause.*) Simply gaze before me with compressed lips. (*Long pause while she does so. No more plucking.*) Not another word as long as I draw breath, nothing to break the silence of this place. (*Pause.*) Save possibly, now and then, every now and then, a sigh into my lookingglass. (*Pause.*) Or a brief . . . gale of laughter, should I happen to see the old joke again. (*Pause. Smile appears, broadens and seems about to culminate in a laugh when suddenly replaced by expression of anxiety.*) My hair! (*Pause.*) Did I brush and comb my hair?

The old joke? Beneath Winnie's engagingly contradictory and distractable persistence, we can't fail to sense an unspoken horror. But the slow-motion farce that is so meticulously scored in the text makes it hard to know exactly what lies behind that naively deliberate, or deliberately naive, *persona*. Who looks through the mask of Winnie's "happy days"? A more poignantly perceptive Winnie? The actress? Beckett himself?

In the second act the mound has risen to Winnie's neck, her
man has now fallen completely silent, her memories are more
fragmentary and banal, and her stories probe yet more painfully the half-hidden wound of solitude. She finally speaks of
little Milly, who crept under the table to dress her dolly:

> Suddenly a mouse. . . . (*Pause.*) Suddenly a mouse ran
> up her little thigh and Mildred, dropping Dolly in her
> fright, began to scream—(*WINNIE gives a sudden pierc-
> ing scream*)—and screamed and screamed—(*WINNIE
> screams twice*)—and screamed and screamed and screamed
> and screamed till all came running, in their night attire,
> papa, mamma, Bibby and . . . old Annie, to see what was
> the matter . . . (*pause*) . . . what on earth could possibly
> be the matter. (*Pause.*) Too late. (*Pause.*) Too late.
> (*Long pause. Just audible.*) Willie.

What *is* the matter? The precisely controlled hysteria of that
scream articulates all the horror implicit in Winnie's situation. Surely her inane and self-conscious rituals have at least
been acts of courageous self-deception? Through her profound
superficiality, her hopeless hope, has she been heroically
playing "happy days" in the face of nothingness? But if so,
can courage still be meaningful in this meaningless world? Is
nothingness perhaps the illusion?

Whether Winnie's play is heroic farce or farcical heroism,
it seems a rich image of our existence stripped to objective
essentials. "When we want fantasy, we do Brecht," Jan Kott
has quipped; "when we want realism, we do Beckett." But of
course Beckett himself understands that realistic art is a "grotesque fallacy" and that the doctrine of *mimesis* is a pretext
for getting rid of the play and dwelling on an illusory abstraction called its "meaning." The whimsical contradictions and
reticent poetry of *Happy Days* resist the application of that
doctrine as strongly as they invite it. The script even proposes
a *"very pompier trompe-l'oeil backcloth."* Why that mocking
temptation? Partly because it requires us to experience something like Winnie's own uncertainty about the status of her
world. Her strangely constructed days, with their relative

nothingness that is always a gratifying something, now reach
out to include us. Do we indignantly dismiss that banal but
riddling artifice, that knowingly theatrical reality? If so, we
are rather like those Showers or Cookers whom Winnie remembers or invents, staring at her and demanding to know
what she *means* but refusing to see that normal Philistine
bipeds may constitute in their willed insensitivity an even
stranger and emptier world. By so trapping us, *Happy Days*
avoids a final commitment to its merely apparent image of life
and yet expands that image to include the action of performance itself. Are playwright, actors, and audience engaged in a
possibly meaningless confrontation with the possibly meaningless?

The question remains a question. But our laughter cannot
now confirm us in a Bergsonian superiority to the mechanical
world at which we laugh. Do we join the playwright in shaping
and controlling this obviously artistic construct? Are we the
Fate that rings the off-stage bell, re-supplies the props, and
drives this indefinitely repeated action? If so, we are doing no
more than Winnie does when she invents a Milly or largely
invents Willie and herself. In fact, we seem much less human
than she as we sit securely in our seats, vicarious devils in
charge of her hell or demiurges responsible for her intense
life. "Yes," she says in Act 1, "the feeling more and more
that if I were not held—" (and she gestures toward the mound
in which she is embedded) "—in this way, I would simply
float up into the blue." Is that where we are? This play won't
let us off the hook. Comic impotence, authentic heroism, and
meaningless or diabolical or creative mastery blend in our
ambiguous role-playing of ambiguous role-playing. We're all
in it together.

But what is the full meaning of this play? Suppose we are
seated at the Royal Court, attending a 1969 revival of Roger
Blin's production of the French version, *Oh les beaux jours*.
On stage, the top half of her body protruding from a canvas-
covered mound, Madeleine Renaud is playing Winnie's comic
and courageous play before the mirror of her own imagination.
As Winnie, rather like some latter-day Monsieur Jourdain in

reduced circumstances, is discovering the meaning of "fully guaranteed genuine pure hog's setae"—that's what she finds so wonderful, some new knowledge every day—Madeleine Renaud is discovering once again, and still freshly, the stylized sub-textual life from which Winnie's words and gestures arise. It is Madeleine Renaud's discovery of Winnie's obtuse shrewdness, empty warmth, and naive and world-weary *élan* that we mirror as we participate in the performance. We therefore experience a delight that Winnie herself cannot know, an immediate comprehension that transforms our merely intellectual bafflement, and an exhilaration that arises not only from the spectacle of a possibly heroic farce amid desolation but also from the almost musically precise enactment of human community.

I don't see that any play can altogether escape such meanings, which inhere as a beneficent irony in the dramatic medium itself. But this script and this production neither hide nor ignore them: they use them boldly. As Madeleine Renaud finds the voice of Winnie talking to herself, she speaks Beckett's muted but precisely cadenced and rigorously scored poetry to *us*—and not just because the script has fixed her there, unalterably facing us. She plays to the audience almost as directly and intimately as if she were giving a farcical monologue by Chekhov in which the phrases came from Maeterlinck's theater of musical stammering. A misreading of a cold text? No. Though a cooler or harsher rendering might also be justifiable, Beckett has said that he couldn't imagine Winnie other than as in Madeleine Renaud's performance. And she is enacting the double paradox at the heart of this play and of all Beckett's work: a shared solitude within an inclusive emptiness. Something of this *is* being heard. And are we too sighing into Winnie's looking-glass?

The script has further uses for that style of playing. '*Étrange sensation*," says Renaud-Winnie during Act 1. "*Étrange sensation, que quelqu'un me regarde.*" She feels that she is clear and dim, back and forth, in and out of someone's eye. Who is looking at her? Perhaps nobody: this may be another self-deception or a compensatory hallucination. But perhaps she feels the absent presence of the hidden god of this play. If that creator or jailer rings the bell, he must also watch her—just as in *Waiting for Godot* someone seems to watch Didi watching Gogo, or as in *Play* the inquisitorial spotlight turns on and off the *dramatis personae*. And yet who can that someone be if not Beckett or his present accomplices in the theater?

When the curtain opens on Act 2, Renaud-Winnie's head alone projects from the canvas, eyes closed. The bell rings. She opens her eyes, greets the light with an apostrophe stolen by Beckett from the blind Milton, closes them again. The bell rings again. Winnie opens her eyes, looks straight at us. A strained smile. Pause. *"Quelqu'un me regarde encore."* Pause. Her eyes still fixed on us. *"Ça que je trouve si merveilleux."* Pause. *"Des yeux sur mes yeux."* Our eyes on her eyes, hers on ours, we take in the meaning of what Renaud-Winnie finds so wonderful: our absent presence, our most ambiguous concern for her.

What image of the human does the play give us in that moment? We are simultaneously victim, author, bell-ringing accomplice, blind voyeur, absent partner, and sensitive player in our cruel and comic and almost heroic play. Since we are also Cookers, we may object to certain contradictions. If our solitude is as final as Winnie's might seem to be, the action of performance is an illusion. If the ambiguities of the play are endless, Madeleine Renaud can't be precisely enacting them in a formal harmony. And if two or more of us *are* gathered together in this way (a phrase on which Winnie herself has faltered), the performed action seems to be perversely gratifying in its willful reduction of our life to emptiness. But the play knows that—just as Hamm does in *Endgame* when he implicitly compares himself to the mad painter who gazed at the rising corn and the sails of the herring fleet and saw only ashes. *Happy Days* invites us to share the void that Winnie must endure, her head full of cries, to share our morally dubious relation to the void and the cries, and to share the plenitude we find in the dramatic medium itself. And finally it invites us to celebrate the strange fact that we can do so.

Our moment of absent meeting with Winnie, of course, isn't the end. Willie himself will become, or almost become, our

ironic surrogate. Speechless and possibly deaf, he crawls downstage and enters Winnie's field of vision. Is he amorous?
murderous? suicidal? Those questions remain questions. He
tries to climb up to her—or to the revolver Brownie—but
slithers back. Then he brings himself to almost inaudible
speech: "Win." That word of loss is enough to give Winnie
her happy day—for a moment. She sings her canned song of
love, the Waltz Duet from the *Merry Widow*, and closes her
eyes. She is now her own music box. Or is she curs? The bell
rings insistently. She opens her eyes, looks straight at us, and
smiles. Then turns her eyes to Willie. Smile off. They look at
each other. Acting and witnessing that look, we contemplate
our own double image. And we know something of the questionable complexity in which we are playing.

WHAT can I conclude about such reflexive playing? Is *Happy
Days* what Lionel Abel some years ago called "metatheatre"?
Not exactly. As Abel understands it, the major development
in Renaissance and post-Renaissance drama results from the
theater's recognition that the life it imitates is already theatrical. Beckett's work is an instance of that development. But
what does Abel mean by "playing"? In "metatheatre" the self-
referring characters, afraid of being mere playthings of unknown forces, become their own playwrights and leading actors. They try to shape themselves and others into plays that
can defy death, project their own designs on the surrounding
darkness, or at least pass the time. Though Abel's description
contains a good deal of truth, it refers almost entirely to a
presumably objective field of play. His model of playing is
essentially manipulative. But as we witness and act *Happy
Days*, we know that its meaning transcends the fiat of its self-
referring character. Abel hasn't seen how the play itself, the
apparent "imitation" of theatrical life, is our present playing in
the intersubjective field.

Is *Happy Days* what Tom Driver, in his recent book *Romantic Quest and Modern Query*, has called "theatrical positivism"? Again, not entirely. For Driver the main development

in modern drama results from the theater's skeptical and alienated withdrawal to the point where it can take only itself as
positive datum. Beckett's work is the epitome and probable
end of that development. But what does Driver mean by
"playing"? In "theatrical positivism" drama becomes a consciously theatrical act rather than an imitation of life—and it
thereby presents an image of life in which consciousness is
imprisoned within itself, going through meaningless routines.
That description also contains a good deal of truth—but again
at the cost of referring almost entirely to a presumably objective
field. Though Driver can elsewhere plead for the histrionic
sensibility as a way of understanding, he here regards playing
in itself as essentially an arbitrary action amid the unknown.
His definition of the theater's positive datum ignores the fact
that any play occurs within our intersubjective field. *Happy
Days* transcends the illuminated circle of solipsist consciousness
—and within our play we know that its meaning can't be di-
vorced from that fact.

At crucial points both Abel and Driver assume that playing
is fundamentally nothing but willful imposition or meaningless
activity. But, if so, how can the play that *presents* such playing
find or convey its meaning? Neither critic sufficiently recognizes
that our playing is always a process of exploration, participation, and celebration—even when the game we play seems to
deny it. Have they been momentarily taken in by our game of
Absence? If life is only theater, it nevertheless moves toward
self-discovery. And if theater is only itself, it nevertheless
knows a sharable life. Any playing that holds the mirror up to
playing can't fail to recognize its own strange powers. And
rejoice in them. Because he who plays the player finds those
powers to be inexplicable gifts.

~~~~~~~~~~~~~~

ARE these notes unfolding the obvious? If so, the obvious is
just what we skillfully hide from ourselves as soon as we try
to extract from a play its apparent statement, its "imitated"
action, or its presented world, and call *that* the "meaning."
And mustn't we now face the fact that such critical surgery,

which constitutes the main procedure in almost all commentary on drama, has tempted us to misconstrue the import of the dominant tradition that runs from Ibsen to Beckett? For the major plays in that tradition don't simply set before us statements of ironic incapacity, inauthenticity, or solipsism. They don't merely "imitate" actions that are increasingly self-defeating, factitious, or meaningless. Nor do they merely present worlds in which human community is present only fitfully or by negation. The major plays in that tradition allow playing to pursue itself into what it implicitly understands to be an illusory cul-de-sac—from which playing *is* the secret exit.

What happens in such plays? As actors and witnesses, moving through a precisely orchestrated event that would be impossible except for our potential ability to engage in authentic reflection and response, we explore the play's masks of paralyzing doubt, desperate impotence, evasion of reciprocity, or total isolation. Grounded in a realm of mutual inclusion, we playfully explore the meaning of the ego's obsessive and contradictory effort to posit itself as an "objective" subject. Through an ironic and purgative miming of our chronic absence, we at least tacitly celebrate our presence to each other in mutuality. Can that be the negative way of our quite secular theater?

Surely the ambiguity central to such playing is inseparable from that which inheres in the "person." Who am I? The speech that enables me to ask that question is grounded in a spontaneous and pre-reflective play—a participatory miming that began long before "I" emerged to self-awareness and that continues subliminally in every action. But the new word "I" has signalled the possibility of a strangely self-absenting play in the field of objects. Can I say "I" without making a fallacious claim to be an independent agent? Can I think of myself or describe myself without constructing a fiction? And can this "I," this self-objectifying person or mask so anxious to continue, so driven to impose its own order on experience, ever find anything new? Can "I" ever change? Musn't "I" rather get lost in another kind of playing, both chosen and spontaneous—a dropping of the old mask and a fresh masking, an acceptance of the unknown and an implicit or even anonymous celebration of presence? If this is still the playing of an "I," it's that of an intersubjective I—no entity but a relational center opening upon the pre-reflective. And yet a moment later won't another objectifying "I" try to possess itself and its world—that is, to remove itself from itself and the world? Won't I once more pretend to *be* somebody? Playing is no more equivocal than I am. If I claim to be here, I'm probably absent; if I let myself disappear, we may be present. Because finally I can *be* no object at all—and not even a separate individual. I can only become, in self-abandonment, an aspect or dimension of community.

Drama, I suspect, always explores our equivocal condition. And the negative way of modern drama is a fresh masking devoted to disclosing among us the inauthenticity of our usual masks—our apparent identity as "persons." Ibsen's *Wild Duck*, for instance, doesn't endorse Dr. Relling's defensive assertion that we must live by life-lies. Nor does it join Gregers Werle in his self-deceptive unmasking of such lies. Ibsen's mirror of our habitually histrionic behavior invites us to play those players—and our playing is of another order. Even a "realistic" play must therefore be understood as a limited kind of participatory drama, the full meaning of which emerges from the ironic relations between the action of the characters that is performed on stage and our present action of performance itself. As such plays become more complex and coherent, those relations tend to become more elaborate and self-reflective. The plays can then begin to interpret their own participatory gestures—including their paradoxical invitation for us to pretend that we aren't there. In *Rosmersholm*, I suspect, Ibsen's kind of "realism" becomes quite fully reflexive. Doesn't that play bring into focus the similarities between our position as impossibly absent witnesses and that which the spying characters try to attain? But doesn't it also bring into focus the differences between their manipulative notion of "taking action" and the understanding of action that inheres in our discovery of their roles? And in *Three Sisters* doesn't Chekhov's kind of "realism" also become quite fully reflexive? Doesn't it bring into focus the contrast between the histrionic self-closure of its characters and our panoramic openness to their roles—the contrast between their chronic deafness and our heightened alertness to the contrapuntal dramatic music? The play itself may therefore enact some answers to those questions that the philosophizing characters are always asking.

In the plays of Pirandello, Genet, and Beckett, our awareness of the participatory dimension seems to have become obsessively articulate—but that's partly an illusion of our negative game. We are now invited to become a bog, a spotlight, actors, or even an audience, and we play a limited role in the action performed—which may seem an image of the performance itself. But we always participate beyond such explicit role-playing and often in contradiction to it. The truth of our mutual presence now lies even more riddlingly in our playful absence.

The opening gesture of Pirandello's *Henry IV* recognizes that we're going to witness ourselves playing playing. As the curtain rises, two actors jump hastily into position: young men who play valets for a player king. And at the end of this enactment of life as a grotesque *commedia dell' arte*, after Belcredi has been stabbed by one who understands the hypnotic inauthenticity of every mask except his own rage against masks, that nameless man will call his attendants around him: "here we are . . . together . . . forever!" But we will say those words with him and through him. And if we share his sense of entrapment, it is because his solitary and enraged inauthenticity is the field of our exploratory play.

The opening gesture of Genet's *Balcony* also recognizes that we're going to witness ourselves playing playing. A mirror on the studio wall reflects an unmade bed that seems in the first rows of the orchestra. Already we find ourselves in a fake brothel where an actor wearing cothurni plays a client who is playing the role of a bishop for an audience of accomplices. And at the end of this enactment of life as the diabolical pursuit of the hypnotic image of impotence, after the iconoclastic rebel has seemed to castrate himself and the Chief of Police has entered the Mausoleum Studio that is said to reflect his image to infinity, the player Queen will dismiss her aides, reveal the mask of Irma behind that of the Queen, and the mask of an actress behind that of Irma, and tell us to "go home, where everything—you can be quite sure—will be falser than here." But her admonition recognizes that, though the *dramatis personae* lust for the fake, our collaborative playing intends a relative truth. In fact, no performance of *The Balcony* would be possible without that intention, which opens to us the meaning of the play itself. Perhaps, as the fake Bishop asserts, the Devil is the great Actor—but in disclosing himself he must pay tribute to the source he denies. A deceptive Absence can play among us only in tacit recognition that its hidden ground is Presence.

WHEN we play the player, every histrionic No masks a commitment to a more difficult Yes. But it's hard to unfold an implicit Yes without deceiving ourselves, and especially hard in a time when the intellect is so ready to indulge in reductive assertions. Perhaps the negative way has justly dominated the modern theater. And perhaps these notes should end right here. But surely there is also an affirmative way? And surely it is no opponent of the negative but a necessary complement? Let this final note play with these questions.

Where does playing the player unfold its own paradoxical gifts? I think here of no coherent tradition but some quite various plays—of Synge's *Playboy of the Western World*, for instance, with its grotesquely lyric questioning of our self-deceptive and yet heuristic playfulness—a playfulness that culminates in Christopher Mahon's realization of manhood and simultaneous disappearance from our stage. Or Ugo Betti's *Queen and the Rebels*, with its contest between the inauthentic mask of nihilism and the authentic mask of the Queen, which here leads the prostitute toward a redemption coincident with death. Or Claudel's *Break of Noon*, where a dialectic of erotic masking and unmasking leads the protagonist toward the crucifying discovery of his true name. In such plays the analogies between the action performed and our action of performance contain fewer dissonances and fuller harmonies. And the paradox of our explicit absence and tacit presence now turns on itself: the fullness of affirmed presence in these plays coincides with apparent annihilation.

Not that plays of this kind must be "superior" to those that follow the negative way. They may easily be less satisfying as aesthetic forms, or less powerful or probing as enactments of our experience. But they do invite us to unfold within the performed action some of the tacit meanings that necessarily reside in our shared action of performance. And if, as sometimes occurs, they also incorporate some major elements of our negative theater, they can become unusually comprehensive mirrors of that playing by which we know ourselves to be human.

Nor do such plays need to share any obvious elements of "doctrine" or traits of "style." Indeed, I think of two plays that seem antithetical in those respects: Hofmannsthal's *Tower* and Brecht's *Causasian Chalk Circle*. Does their "meaning" reside in their ostensible statements? If so, a Christian pessimism stands against a Marxist optimism. Or in their styles? If so, a late romantic symbolism stands against an ironically rational parable, or the baroque opulence of Reinhardt against the indicated realism of the Berliner Ensemble. Yet both *The Tower* and *The Caucasian Chalk Circle* are, in effect, modern festival dramas. Each is also, in its own way, a reflexive play-within-a-play, aware of our emptily destructive role-playing and of the problematic nature of community in our time, but also aware that actors can explore for us and with us the major issues of an essentially dramatic life. This affinity wouldn't have surprised either playwright. More than two decades after Hofmannsthal had introduced *Baal* in a vein of wry respect, Brecht was sketching a *Salzburg Dance of Death* that might have been a successor to Hofmannsthal's *Everyman*. And *The Caucasian Chalk Circle* itself plays variations on the adaptation of the chalk-circle parable that Klabund had made in 1924 for Reinhardt. It is that commitment to participatory playing, I suspect, which keeps *The Tower* from sinking into religious allegory and takes *The Caucasian Chalk Circle* well beyond the political fantasy of its prologue. These two plays invite us to find not opposed but complementary meanings in our shared commitment to playing the player.

Each moves toward a Shakespearean wholeness, composed of mutually illuminating modes of playing. It is no accident that Hofmannsthal re-imagines the works of Calderón and Grimmelshausen with the help of *King Lear*, and that Brecht re-imagines Klabund's play and his Eastern parable with the help of festive comedy. And at the center of both *The Tower* and *The Caucasian Chalk Circle* stand roles—not persons but roles—through which we can explore what may happen when we give ourselves to that fresh playing which culminates in a simultaneous affirmation and annihilation. The final tableau of *The Tower* (in the version of 1927) bears witness to the Sigismund who has been led, through his preconscious commitment to life's dreamplay, beyond the brutalizing roles of power politics into an awareness that all is vanity except the conversation of spirit with spirit, and who in the friendly gesture that brings his death has found his true role. And the final dance of *The Caucasian Chalk Circle* enacts our participation in the fertile energy of Azdak, who has been led, through his expedient and exuberant improvisations, beyond our more venal and vicious masking to the discovery of his true role as ironic lord of misrule, the just judge, and who must now disappear.

—*And that's my cue. Do you take yourself for another Azdak? How could you hope to demonstrate those outrageous claims? Perhaps* Rosencrantz & Guildenstern Are Dead *and* Happy Days *do enact some paradoxes of playing the player. But does* The Wild Duck? *Or* Rosmersholm? *I can't see that Ibsen's realism implies any kind of reflexive or participatory drama. And your quaintly negative and affirmative ways just sidestep all the stylistic differences that separate Chekhov from Genet or Hofmannsthal from Brecht. How can so general an approach ever arrive at the unique whatness of a particular play? Is this supposed to be an essay in dramatic criticism?*

—With your help, perhaps. Have you forgotten or do you deny my major assumption?

—*Namely?*

—That a play's meaning must include the meaning of our participation in its playing.

—*Even if the play itself denies that assumption?*

—Even if the play's most easily describable action seems to conflict with that assumption. The full meaning of every play, whatever themes its characters may illustrate or expound, resides in the form of our shared acting-and-witnessing. Certainly that form can include dissonances between the "imitated" or performed action and our present action of performance. But can a play deny its medium?

—*Playwrights can and do ignore what you think is implied by the medium. Why else have we spent so much energy in the last few decades breaking out of the proscenium stage?*

—We've had to *break* out of that stage because we had already reduced its action by our habitually objectifying thought. That's why the simple step of opening things up—a step with which I have a great deal of sympathy—has required so much energy and has so often led to a boring chaos in the name of "participatory theater." Even so intelligent a director as Richard Schechner can talk about a scripted play as if it were a closed object entirely external to us. After that academic reduction, what can he do but look for ingenious ways of getting us *back into* the play? When we visit the Performing Garage, we may sometimes be grateful for the results of his quixotic misunderstanding. But that shouldn't hide the fact that a masterpiece of Ibsen's middle period implicitly understands its full participatory meaning much better than do those critics or directors who have attacked or *defended* its "realism."

—*Nonsense. Your major assumption is just a way of begging the whole question. What you call the "full meaning" of a play is simply a set of contradictions between the meaning in the usual sense—that of what you call the "performed action" —and the meaning you choose to find in the "action of performance."*

—Not so simply. Any powerful and comprehensive play is surely alert to its primary commitments, whatever the playwright's conscious intent. Its full meaning is therefore likely to contain not unresolved contradictions but analogies or at least thematically central paradoxes that are elucidated by its own total form.

—*Show me.*

—Well, let me start by trying to formulate three hypotheses that might stand in opposition to that critical surgery by which we usually extract from a play its apparent statement, its "imitated" action, or its presented world.

First: The meaning of any work of art emerges from the interaction between what it seems to present and what it *is* as a presentation, somewhat as the meaning of a fresh metaphor emerges from the interaction between its mutually illuminating terms. A poem's full meaning therefore includes the relations between the fiction that it speaks and its action of poetic speaking. And a play's full meaning must include the relations between its polar terms, the action performed and the action of performance.

Second: The more coherent the play, the more it brings into focus analogies between those terms. Then the *dramatis personae* and the participants in the dramatic event begin to share by analogy in the play's "spine" or "action."

—*Wait a minute. You want to borrow the analytic scheme that Francis Fergusson used in* The Idea of a Theater *and extend it to cover the whole dramatic event?*

—With whatever changes such an extension to our inclusive and participatory form might require.

—*But how about the indeterminacy of each participant's action and thought? Surely we participate in many ways— and our consciousness of that participation must be indefinitely variable. How can you seriously speak of "analogies" between the action performed and the action of performance?*

—How can we speak of the "meaning" of the performed action itself, when we know that actors, directors, and critics may debate it endlessly? Only on the assumption that our relation to the play, as to any act of communication, though always remaining incomplete and therefore partly obscure, is nevertheless telic: that it is oriented *toward* a more coherent and complete understanding. Otherwise we are lost in the arbitrary. We begin, of course, in relative diversity and confusion.

But we can move toward harmony and clarity. Only on that assumption can the director and the cast prepare a production. In witnessing the play, and in understanding our participation in it, we can make the same assumption. No doubt our initial and inadequately prepared experiences of the dramatic event always include a great deal of arbitrariness and blindness. And we will always be tempted to find our merely private analogies to the performed action. But if we remain open to the play, the most appropriate elements in our action of performance will gradually be brought into prominence by the force of the analogical field itself. Every major script is therefore a verbal invitation that elicits a movement toward a distinctively harmonious dramatic event: *that* is what you called a moment ago its "unique whatness."

—*But even if that were true, how could a critic possibly speak or write about such a various and mainly tacit movement?*

—Certainly the process itself would be much more difficult to speak of than that of reading a poem. And the normative or ideal *end* of that process, which we might call the action of the "implied actors and witnesses," would also be more difficult to speak of than the action of a poem's "implied reader." And yet, with the help of fictive paradigms, perhaps we can try to do all these things.

That's why I said we would need some changes in critical procedure. Objective analysis from a fixed and external point of view would be a self-contradictory mistake. As participants we are always quite variously on the way toward understanding how characters, actors, and witnesses share by analogy in a unified but multivocal action. In order to speak *of* and *from* our movement along that way, we would need an exposition that is dialogical and frankly incomplete. And we would need to speak *through* a variety of critical fictions. The results of such criticism would not be final propositions about plays: each fiction would have to contain qualifying ironies that would prevent us from simply identifying it with the experience of which it seems to speak. After all, no fiction can ever assert the final truth about existence. A fiction provides at best a more richly adequate verbal filter or a more sharply focusing but astigmatic lens for us to see through on the next pertinent occasion. Such criticism as I propose might likewise prepare us for a more intense and complete participation in the whatness of each particular play—and so lead us a little further toward that almost unimaginable condition in which we *are* both the play and the players.

But I had a third hypothesis: As the action performed and the action of performance illuminate each other through analogy, the play begins to articulate the meaning of its own style, its own distinctive world of symbolic forms.

—*Come now, that's carrying your preference for contemporary reflexiveness too far! Every major play, whatever its style, is finally about itself?*

—Every major play, whatever its style, begins to discover how it necessarily is about its own specific form of playing. After all, the works in every art explore the meanings that are potential in their given medium. Plays are no exception. The medium of dramatic events is the realm of mutual participation as we can know it through our chronic estrangement. And as the plays of our apparently centerless modern theater discover that fact through their own forms of playing, they move in unique ways toward a common ground of presence.

—*And no doubt their actions all then become versions of your formula "to play the player."*

—You laugh, but why not? That's no reduction to the absurd but the true end of playing.

—*How so?*

—Because it means the playful undoing of that objectifying "I" which is my usual histrionic self. What happens when "I" am completely undone by play?

—*How could I possibly know?*

—Exactly. And what can I do but playfully ask? Shall we test those hypotheses?

—*Only if we can begin with a play that is realistic, non-reflexive, and non-participatory.*

—Then you will have to name it.

—*Begin with Ibsen.* Rosmersholm.

THREE

KILLING
OURSELVES

—All right. Can we agree that *Rosmersholm* has abandoned
those conventions of the well-made play which detract from
the power of *A Doll's House* and *Ghosts?* That Ibsen's "realism" has here become a quite fully defined angle of vision?

—*Agreed. The action no longer seems to address us. We're
outside the play, inferring its meaning. No participation, no
reflexiveness.*

—But don't the characters also tend to be external and
analytic observers of each other?

—*Of course. Each part of the play's world must be as objective and problematic for them as the whole is for us.*

—But doesn't that fact increase our identification with them
—and our reciprocity with those who act them for us?

—*What are you getting at?*

—Though we seem "outside the play," it reaches out to include us. And as we act and witness "observing the observers,'
the play articulates for us the meaning of its own apparent style.

—*Which is?*

—The play's final moments will disclose what has been the
characters' deepest secret, and ours: a commitment to suicide.

—*Ridiculous! The suicide of John Rosmer and Rebecca
West doesn't result from any such earlier commitment—and
it certainly doesn't implicate us. They leap off the bridge into
the mill-race because they can't free themselves from the past.
Rosmer's liberal ideas have been undercut by his conservative
temperament. Rebecca's spirit has been "ennobled" and her
will broken by the Rosmer tradition. And both of them are
overwhelmed by guilt. Rosmer now knows that he has been,
in effect, a tacit accomplice in Rebecca's tempting of Beata*

*toward suicide. And Rebecca, who is guilty enough on that
score, is also stunned by the probability that she has committed incest with Dr. West. Through suicide these two now
judge themselves, atone for their sins, and join each other in
marriage. For freethinkers who can't escape their Lutheran
heritage, it's an ironic but radiant catastrophe—a nearly tragic
resolution.*

—Of course you're right, from their own declared point of
view. But how can we accept their explanations and judgments?
Characters within Ibsen's "realism" can say no more than they
let themselves understand, and in fact Rebecca says much less.
Her fourth-act confession won't square at all with her earlier
complicated behavior. Let's not make the usual mistake of
interpreting this play in terms of the ideas that the characters
talk about—emancipation, nobility, tradition, a broken will,
and so forth. Our infatuation with the "idea" is just what Ibsen
questions, here and elsewhere. Ideas are masks. And the nature
of mask-wearing emerges in action. If we don't see that, we
remain with Ibsen the ideologue and lose the dramatist who
put that ideologue through ironic ordeals, in successive drafts
of the same play and in successive plays on the same theme.

—*The ideas here are just symptoms of a hidden reality? Do
you agree with Freud's view that Rebecca's experiences at
Rosmersholm result from the Oedipus complex? That she is
trapped by the incest-fantasy which she has already acted out
with her mother and Dr. West?*

—Freud too was right, from an analytic point of view that
the play also tempts us to adopt. When Ibsen's characters explain their present life as a function of the past, we're easily
led to join them. Freud could even praise the "analytical perspi-
cacity" of that defensive and reactionary schoolmaster, Kroll.
But the ideas in this play are not symptoms of a causally determined condition: they are masks of present intentions. And
though Freud's own account of Rebecca's past is certainly more
dispassionate than Kroll's, it is still far from adequate to the
play's present action, which in fact assesses our impulse to engage in any such reductive causal analysis.

—*How so?*

—Bernard Shaw once said, "In the theatre of Ibsen . . . we are 'guilty creatures sitting at a play.' " He spoke even better than he knew. *Rosmersholm* is just such a "Mousetrap" as a modern Hamlet might provide: a play that tempts us to collaborate with the most evident principle of its characters' thought and its own style, and then confronts us with the meaning of that collaboration.

—*Our secret commitment to suicide? But that's a meaning you still haven't produced.*

—The play leads us to discover that Rosmer and Rebecca, those sensitive idealists who speak of mutuality, of "laying hold on life," of gaining the "great world of truth and freedom," really want something quite different. Implicit in their action, moment by moment, is a secret aim that they won't admit even to themselves. We soon recognize that aim in other characters, too—and in ourselves. For *Rosmersholm* focuses on the paradox that Ibsen's ' realism," as a stylistic perspective and as our habitual mode of constituting the world, means no genuine engagement with the real but a flight from it—a quest for absence. In disclosing that meaning, *Rosmersholm* becomes a kind of participatory drama—its "realistic" mimicry a symbolic miming, its "objective" spectacle a poetry of shared acting-and-witnessing. We must try to imagine a performance. For the play says to us what Rebecca will say to Rosmer late in Act 4, with the almost imperceptible smile of an accomplice who understands the temptation offered: "Come with me—and witness—"

⚹⚹⚹⚹⚹⚹⚹⚹⚹⚹⚹⚹

THE house-lights go down, the curtain opens, and we occupy the place we have always wanted. Liberated from human space, subject to no claim or call, we observe beyond the invisible fourth wall a boxed-in material world that doesn't recognize our existence. We join in the illusion that there is no illusion, that from this vantage-point of an impossible self-negation we can observe the "real." What a delightfully Cartesian world it is! We are disembodied heads observing the objective space and time of the world's body.

But what do we see? A comfortable but potentially claustral space; a cold stove decorated with signs of new life; military and ecclesiastical portraits gazing in from the walls; a window and doors giving on an inviting but settled prospect; and a woman, somewhere between fresh youth and established maturity, who sits by the window crocheting a large white shawl that is nearly finished. That ambiguous image of old life and new, opening and closure, prepares us to see beneath the "realistic" surfaces. The play will tacitly speak to us *through* its apparent objects. And a silent action now prepares us to see mirrored on stage our own surface mode of witnessing: Rebecca peeps out of the window from behind the flowers. She too is a momentarily "liberated" consciousness (masking herself behind the image of new life, but in a closed room, watched over by pictures of death) who wants to observe something that will be unaware of her existence. Though we don't yet realize it, the actress who mimes Rebecca also mimes us.

When Mrs. Helseth enters, that analogy extends itself. She acts at once in behalf of our post of observation. Her questions probe the scene: "Isn't it draughty there, miss?" "A little. Would you close it please?" Politely masked spying; politely masked defense. On that conventional level the play's main business now begins within the stage-box: the thrust and parry of characters each of whom tries to remain hidden behind some curtained window while interpreting and manipulating an external action. Their brief moments of rapport are moments of collaboration in that enterprise—as now: "Why, isn't that the Pastor coming now?" "Where? . . . Yes, that's him. . . . Get back. Don't let him see us." And they watch Rosmer fail to cross the bridge into "new life"—a bridge we'll finally see as the bridge to death.

Before Rosmer reaches the house, Kroll enters as a more skillful spy than Mrs. Helseth and a more complex agent on our behalf. He politely sounds the relation between Rebecca and Rosmer, denies the import of his own safely withdrawn position against Rebecca's counterspying, and yet exhibits an obscure urge to confess. We'll soon see that he also wants to pull Rosmer into the circle of his own point of view. Rebecca's motives in this scene are similar. Though we don't yet see her manipulation of Rosmer, her rejection of a life genuinely *with* him, or her urge to confess, we do see that she is masking her inner life from others and herself. Along with an obvious role-playing (of warmth, casualness, puzzlement, modesty) to protect herself from Kroll, she engages in a more self-deceptive pretence of fresh innocence and of mutuality with Rosmer. Why has she decorated the room with all these flowers? *She must be on the side of life.* And we follow her shifting answers to Kroll's comments on that compensatory excess—from matter-of-fact evasion ("Mr. Rosmer loves to have fresh flowers around") to the partial admission of involvement ("Yes. I find them so beautifully soothing") and a recovery of balance in quiet self-justification ("In the old days we had to deny ourselves that pleasure"). The same masking appears in her modest but tense answer to Kroll's question about marriage ("I have the place I want, Dr. Kroll") and in her ensuing agitation.

In this context, Ibsen's "retrospective analysis" isn't just an expository technique: it is a mode of action that we share with the characters as we try to construct from external observation the hypothetical shape of an off-stage past. And like James's *Aspern Papers* or *The Sacred Fount*, this play explores the meaning of its own apparent point of view. Each character wants to be absent from the field he analyzes—to be outside a box looking in. But each is also disclosed to others as inside a box. Perhaps no play more fully examines the situation that Sartre, who has never escaped his Cartesian heritage, would later assert to be essential to the relations between consciousnesses: the Medusa gaze of subjects who perceive each other as objects. It's a very short step from this room in Rosmersholm to the hell of *No Exit*. This mode of witnessing, imagined by each as a means of liberation, is ironically an act of self-enclosure. And that contradiction leads to another. For each major character, to act is to manipulate certain human objects so as to bring them into his or her own citadel of absence. The ostensible end, rather like that of a Sartrean project for a "We," is a new life in freedom, innocence, and mutuality. But because the means preserve the split between subject and object, the end is a mirage. Scene by scene, the play shows the movement toward that mirage and implicates us in it.

By the end of Act 2, of course, we'll see Rebecca's contradictory impulses rise to the surface in her threatening but secretly yearning rejection of Rosmer's proposal. But at this early point in the play, while we're still mainly interested in Rosmer, she is the most ambiguous agent of our own post of observation. When Rosmer enters, she seems little more than an observer—drawing out Rosmer and Kroll, encouraging them, illuminating the scene while keeping herself out of it. Her repeated business with the lamp at moments of tension is a key gesture: she masks herself by shedding light on something else. But suddenly from behind Kroll's back she urges Rosmer to declare himself; and when he resists, she tries to force him to do so. She hints that he has "come to look at life from a more liberal view-point than before," draws from Kroll a fuller statement of intention, and then threatens to reveal everything—using the appearance of candor as a device to make Rosmer speak candidly.

The entrance of Brendel interrupts her only for a moment. She pointedly admires that former tutor's bold declaration of purpose—and then leaves the room with him (overruling Rosmer's own invitation) so that Rosmer is left alone with Kroll. This strategy links her even more closely to us: as Rosmer finally declares himself to Kroll, we observe her success from an absent vantage point that she would relish. And as we now grasp what has been her intent, aren't our sympathies mainly with her? She has been urging Rosmer to step toward independence and mutuality, and he is now glad to have done so. We've shared in her desire to remain in darkness while watching him act with the candor she admires and so "join" her in a position that she has never really occupied.

At the same time, we share Rosmer's own relation to the world. He too wants to remain hidden while rousing others from the "outside" to liberate their minds and purify their wills. And despite a conscious integrity, he subtly uses the woman by whom he is used. He can stand forth to declare himself openly—as he puts it—only because he is led by a

subordinate who acts boldly in behalf of his inhibited yearn-
ings. But if she manipulates him through his desire to be manipulated, he dominates her through his dependence. Mirror-
ing each other, they will lock themselves into an embrace they
never understand.

But Brendel has already begun to help us understand it. That
pretentious parasite also intends to "abandon the role of modest onlooker," "descend into the arena of life," and "proceed
to action" in behalf of freedom. But he too really wants to
"savour things in solitude"—to hide himself from others and
himself, while fixing the identity of others and manipulating
them. In his comic floridity, he is an ironic mirror of Rosmer
and Rebecca. And as he exposes the empty heart of this play's
objectifying world, he begins to transcend its "realistic" texture.
Brendel's histrionic emptiness elicits from the actor a broad
style of playing, which pierces all "realistic" conventions to
remind us that we are indeed *playing* such a world. And when
Brendel returns to the stage in Act 4, no longer merely ludi-
crous but grotesquely sinister, he will reveal his emptiness to
be death itself.

Let's speed up a bit. Act 2 further develops the mode of
witnessing that informs this world—and further implicates us
in it. The scene is Rosmer's study, that inner box of his clois-
tered consciousness. First Rebecca visits him to tell of her off-
stage maneuvering. To advance the cause of truth she has sent
Brendel to the editor Mortensgaard with a note that falsely
represents Rosmer's position. Then, after Rebecca leaves, Kroll
reports his suspicions of her—suspicions based on what Beata
has said just before her death. (Mrs. Helseth interrupts this
conversation, of course, asking for Rebecca—an interruption
that we'll later recognize to have contained clues to Rebecca's
present spying.) And then Mortensgaard, having been maneu-
vered by the off-stage Rebecca into a confrontation with Kroll
and Rosmer, enters as one more agent of light (the *Morning
Star*) who spies and manipulates. His "warning" to Rosmer,
based on Beata's letter, is polite revenge on a man who had
once accused him of a moral lapse—and is also a shrewd bit
of political blackmail.

By this time, Rebecca's business with the lamp in Act 1 has become an inclusive metaphor. Each character masks himself by shedding light on others. Each reports on others in order to control. Each is therefore guilty of the "false witness" with which Kroll charges Mortensgaard. In this world of external observation the off-stage past must remain ambiguous: about it we can infer only probabilities. But we can know each character's present response to this problematic situation, and his witnessing is "false" if it is evasive and reductively accusing. Each, in fact, shares by analogy in what Rosmer calls Beata's mode of vision: "always silent, silent—watching us—noting everything—and misinterpreting everything." And each shares in her suicidal self-removal that fastens guilt on others in a "terrible accusing victory."

Kroll and Mortensgaard enact the ordinary versions of such witnessing: the righteous indignation of the fearful and jealous "conservative" and the scandal-mongering of the vindictive and opportunist "liberal." The witnessing of Ibsen's more sensitive idealists is a subtler matter. Rosmer's reconstruction of the past may cause him to face his own aloofness from the passionate Beata—but does he suspect how long he may have contributed to her plight? In any case, he now finds that guilt and despair justify his continuing impulse to absent himself from the scene. And as our collaboration with Rosmer in his retrospective analysis draws us closer to his spectator's view of life, the play drives home our resemblance to Rebecca by a bold mirror effect. After Mortensgaard leaves, she draws open the curtain on the other side of the stage-box. With us, she has spied on almost all that has happened. Despite the claim she will make on the next day, her will to possess the object is far from broken.

The paradoxical climax of Act 2 sums up the predicament of these self-styled "free agents" whose present action always denies the life in mutuality of which they dream. Rosmer sits lost in despair, and Rebecca approaches him *"cautiously from behind"*—as she has effectively been doing throughout the play. When she suggests creating a "new relationship," Rosmer makes a proposal of marriage for which she seems unprepared. We think we understand her sudden joy. But what of her withdrawal? Why does she utter such a final refusal? And why, in spite of that, does she seem to accept Rosmer's prediction that she will "never leave Rosmersholm?"

In Act 4 Rebecca will maintain that this cry of joy arose from her "old spirit and will . . . crying out for their freedom," and that her cry of seeming terror a moment later arose from "despair" over her loss of the "power to take action" now that her will had been enslaved by Rosmersholm's moral nobility. But that isn't what we see. As the actress mimes Rebecca, discovering what's implicit in the stage directions, she is not merely lapsing back into passivity. Both before and after that cry "*as though in terror*"—a cry with a slightly histrionic edge, as she holds her hands to her ears—Rebecca utters a "*controlled*" and "*composed*" refusal. Does her strange self-mastery, or self-blocking, result from guilt at the prospect of taking the place of a woman she has driven to suicide? Or, as Freud argues, from the shame of an unconscious incest-fantasy already enacted and now being compulsively repeated? Guilt was surely evident in her sudden step backward, a moment before, when Rosmer mentioned the need for "innocence." But unless we impose upon all present action the concept of determination by an objectified past, we must admit that guilt in itself doesn't dictate how we will face it. Rather than declaring herself openly, in harmony with her ideals, Rebecca takes a resolute and devious step of a kind that we've seen before. She retreats from the danger of full reciprocity to a position of observing and controlling absence. Guilt doesn't 'wreck her at the moment of attainment," as Freud would have it. Guilt invites her to accelerate the downward spiral of her own moment-by-moment decisions. Still avoiding genuine responsibility, she keeps her hold on Rosmer now by threatening him with the secret end that she has already enacted by implication in every such self-exclusion: "But if you ever ask me that again . . . I shall go the way Beata went."

Those words bring into focus the entire contradictory pattern of Rebecca's impulses: her desire for absolute power and for release from conflict, her self-justification and her secret guilt,

her opposition to Beata and her identification with that absolute image of self-removal. With a portentous "Now you
know"—and with the slow nod of one who wants to hypnotize
herself and her partner—Rebecca leaves. Rosmer stands alone
in his claustral study, staring at the closed door. The ghost of
Beata will now dominate the action.

Acts 3 and 4 make a pattern of "discoveries" and "confessions" through which the characters tempt one another toward
death. The appropriate end—Rosmer's and Rebecca's final endorsement of the purpose that has secretly shaped their entire
action—will be mutual hypnotism in the act of suicide. Kroll,
for instance, brings "truth." Claiming to "have done a little
research" on the question of Rebecca's birth, he accuses her
of illegitimacy while trying to blackmail her into legalizing the
relation to Rosmer that he assumes her to have. In effect, he
tempts her toward death by inadvertently suggesting the possibility of incest. Thinking Kroll's accusation to be correct,
Freud concluded that Rebecca's readiness for suicide results
from the discovery of incest "in actual fact." And it's true that
an earlier draft of the play was firmer on this point. But in
Rosmersholm itself, which is beyond the mechanical contriv-
ances of Holberg or Scribe, such antecedent "facts" can exist
only as the characters' interpretations. For the actress who
mimes Rebecca's agitation, this "discovery" can be no more
than a powerful suspicion awakened by a man who is disturbed
by her ideas and by her erotic power—a suspicion to which
she is already disposed to surrender.

Rosmer also brings "truth." He sees more clearly his responsibility to Beata, his political naiveté, his passion for Rebecca, and Rebecca's own machinations. But again he lets
those insights justify an impulse to run away, to obliterate
himself, and, in the play's closing moments, to establish a
final dependent control over Rebecca. By that time Rebecca
will have also brought "truth." But each of her "confessions"
will have claimed a misleading finality, defended some area of
alleged integrity, and kept her in a position of relative power.

In Act 3 she seems ready to confess rather fully, as Kroll
may suspect, but Rosmer's interruption—"But, Rebecca—I

know all this"—helps to save her from needless revelations. Composing herself, she confesses only what she thinks necessary: nothing about her relation to Dr. West, but rather its surprising psychological analogue, her tempting of Beata. "I knew well where your salvation lay," she says to Rosmer. "Your only hope of salvation. So I took action." In those words each character might rationalize his manipulation of others toward an illusory goal. But despite this confession Rebecca can still rebuff Kroll with vehemence and chilly aloofness. And after Kroll and Rosmer leave, she can spy on them and observe with disguised gratification that Rosmer still fears to cross the bridge. Her will remains in control.

In Act 4 she announces that she will disclose something that puts everything else in its true light. Charging that Rosmersholm has "broken" her will, she says that her love for Rosmer began in the courage of a "free will," passed through uncontrollable passion and selfless tranquillity, and has now declined into paralysis. But at best she is reading back into earlier events the position she may now feel herself to occupy. She blames Rosmersholm for all the guilt arising from her treatment of Beata and from Kroll's accusation. And she hides or ignores the fact that she has deceptively exercised her will up to this very moment. When Rosmer again suggests marriage, she puts him off with another reason: she has a past, something yet "more terrible." But whatever her relation with Dr. West, she doesn't disclose it—partly because Rosmer, with a *"faint smile"* of secrecy, acknowledges that he had suspected something, had "played with the thought," but is now ready to "forget." Are they willing to let the past disappear? Not at all: their action insures its continuing life. For the heart of the matter is their repeated failure to declare themselves. They still continue to want, not the risks of spontaneous mutuality, but the distantly intimate securities of reciprocal domination and dependence.

In moving from Dr. West to Rosmer, Rebecca has defined herself again in terms of a fatherly figure whom she can subtly dominate. She depends upon the paternal order that she finds claustral. And Rosmer, in moving from Brendel to Rebecca— avoiding on the way the passionate demands of Beata—seems to have defined himself again in terms of one whom Rosmers-holm keeps safely subordinate. He relies upon the privileged position that he thinks to abandon. Both of these self-deceptive idealists want simultaneously to control and be controlled, to enclose and be enclosed, and they so produce an increasingly guilt-ridden and self-hypnotic replica of their past. Yet neither is ready to meet the world from within the insecurity of ad-mitted guilt. Partly discovering their failure, they are tempted to take even bolder flight from mutuality—in order to reach a more intensely reciprocal domination and dependence. How can the father who is a child marry the child who is a mother? They want to commit that final double-edged act of will, to murder and be murdered, to wield and to suffer an absolute power, to become both God and nothing, to box in the world and eliminate themselves from the box.

Do they want more than we have wanted? We began by in-dulging our belief that we can know the "real" by reducing it to an order that we observe from the outside. We created our "innocence" by abstracting ourselves from human encounter. We pretended to be gods, but our minds were enclosed by the secure horizon of the order we posited. We forgot that we can know only by sharing a community of interpretation, that we are responsible only as we respond, that we are free only as we are vulnerable. We expected no direct dialogue from the stage to disturb our position. But the play itself reveals the meaning of our desire.

Just before Brendel arrives, Rosmer and Rebecca begin to speak of their "emptiness," each asserting that the other some-how has the key to life, each ready to pull the other into his own death-in-life so that the void may wear the mask of mar-riage. Brendel enters, once again a clarifying image. Now completing the downward arc of his trajectory, he is "home-sick for the great void." He has found that his carefully un-opened box of treasure contained nothing. That comic detail, an apt comment on the would-be artist or political agent, brings into focus the play's larger pattern of empty boxes—those on which we spy, those in which we hide ourselves. And Brendel now warns Rebecca that she can insure Rosmer's success only by chopping off her little finger and cutting off her left ear. That clairvoyant warning, which sparks their final collaboration, has disturbed critics who try to fix the action of *Rosmersholm* in terms of "realistic" and external relations among human objects. For them the only possible witness is the self-removed voyeur. But despite its apparent style, *Rosmersholm* requires us to understand that we are all potentially clairvoyant participants.

When Brendel leaves, Rosmer and Rebecca begin their final scene of temptation. Rebecca isn't, as Hermann Weigand thought, "the wholly will-less instrument of her lover's morbid fantasies." As Rosmer tempts her toward death, she cooperates with his fascinated exercise of power and then effectively dares him, tempts him, to join her. "Yes, John. Come with me—and witness—" And again: "To the bridge, yes. You will never dare to walk on it." Of course she urges him to stay behind; but her surface objections dissolve with the same readiness that he exhibits in joining her. And since he himself had earlier planned death, from which her sacrifice is presumably designed to save him, he has been obliquely tempting her to go to death *with* him, but *ahead* of him, all the while. That's one reason for their inability to say who goes with whom. Rebecca now dares to go all the way Beata went: in a single act she will become the mother and kill the mother, gain control over Rosmer and yield to his control, atone for her destruction of life and destroy life again, commit her final assault on the world and withdraw from it. And Rosmer now dares to go all the way onto the bridge—to be her witness, executioner, and victim. He will put death behind himself by killing himself, gain faith in his power to "ennoble" others from outside by repeating Rebecca's murder of Beata, and join Rebecca at last in an escape from the world he refuses to meet.

Does the rhetoric with which these earnest players mask their ambivalences suggest a tragic or Nietzschean redemption? John Northam has said, "They die with dignity, proving the greatness of humanity when will and conscience combine, but proving also how difficult such a combination is to achieve."

And M. C. Bradbrook has said, "The inevitable is freely chosen; and in this reconcilation of necessity and freedom, in 'joyously' paying the price, Rosmer and Rebekke are freed of their guilt of the past." Surely nothing could be further from the truth. Their talk of expiation and marriage hides a will to *end* all mutuality, all living together with guilt, confession, forgiveness, and freedom. And their joy arises, at its deepest level, from the imminence of that end, the self-produced finality they have always wanted.

Rosmer and Rebecca leave the stage, and for a few moments we look through our curtained aperture upon that empty box. Then Mrs. Helseth enters—domestic object, prudent observer, and unwitting folk-chorus. Perplexed by their absence, she goes to the window and looks out into the darkness. "What's that white thing over there—?" The white shawl, the light of false witness, and the white horses of the obsessively re-enacted past now merge as Rosmer and Rebecca embrace in the outer darkness that makes absolute the emptiness within. "The dead mistress has taken them." Yes—the very spirit of passionately deluded and self-absenting observation. And as we remain fixed on the lighted scene from which we too are absent, we face a paradox. Do we imagine ourselves safely outside that fourth wall, spying upon their death as upon some objective spectacle? If so, that death is also ours: we go with Rebecca as "witnesses" unaware that the very style of *Rosmersholm* has tempted us into a secret complicity. Do we see ourselves in Rosmer and Rebecca, and them in ourselves? If so, we move beyond their death—but only by facing another kind of death at which Ibsen obliquely aimed in many plays, from *Brand* and *Peer Gynt* to *When We Dead Awaken*. Recognizing the contradictory nothingness of the "I" that wants autonomy and security, we understand the need to allow that "I" to lapse. And we therefore understand the double meaning of the Button Molder's remark to Peer Gynt: "To be oneself is: to kill oneself."

Rosmersholm has invited us to mime, both *as* a performance and *within* that performance, our desire to reduce the world to an enclosed and enclosing object. It has invited us to dis-

cover, within our field of observation and so in the very act of
constituting that field, the meaning of our desire. In accepting
that invitation and recognizing its implications, we have com-
pleted the movement toward confession which the characters
of *Rosmersholm* always block or subvert. For we have enacted
our recognition that the optimism founded on the will to know
the object is—as Maritain put it in *The Dream of Descartes*—
"committed to suicide." And we have therefore joined the Ibsen who could say, "I have aimed in every poem or play at
my own spiritual emancipation and purification, for a man
shares in the responsibility and guilt of the age he belongs to."

*—I doubt that. Hasn't your analysis been just as reductive
as Freud's? How can that elaboration of a few analogies do
justice to the richness of the play's characterization, imagery,
and themes?*

—Of course, it can't. There's much more to say about all
those subjects. But surely I've not been as reductive as Freud
—exactly because my analysis is more adequate to the total
form of our playing. I maintain only that *Rosmersholm* can't be
less than I've described: that its total form includes our shared
movement toward absence, and that Ibsen's "realism" articulates through that movement the meaning of its world of
symbolic forms.

*—But why say that we join Ibsen in any confessional inten-
tion? Didn't you earlier suggest that analogies between the
performed action and our action of performance will arise
whenever a play's style attains full definition and each aspect
therefore begins to reflect all the others?*

—For the playwright as for us, such analogies are always
discoveries, and yet they also articulate an implicit intention.
We always act or speak beyond our present understanding.
Each draft of *Rosmersholm* was for Ibsen, as this statement
is for me, a speculative moment in a dialogue with the medium,
through which we intend truth. The meaning of such moments
will unfold as the dialogue proceeds, in accord with the formal
principles of the medium. That's why Ibsen could say, "I do

but ask." For him, ironic questioning was the dominant mode
of confessing the truth. In draft after draft, and in play after
play, his questioning followed a negative dialectic that exposed
limited speculations and suicidal falsehoods for what they are.
In his major work that dialectic explores the closed spaces
that are called into being by our objectifying and self-absenting will. His "realism" is just one phase of that exploration.

   —You'll have to expand that.

   —Think of the protagonists of those neatly antithetical plays,
Brand and *Peer Gynt*. Brand, in whom Ibsen could see his own
"best" qualities, commits himself to a posited Absolute and
defines himself through rigorously selective action. His motto:
"All or Nothing!" What happens? Sacrificing his son Ulf, demanding of his wife Agnes a total devotion to this pseudo-
Kierkegaardian calling, refusing all genuine mutuality, Brand
must be always on the move toward a divine freedom that is
elsewhere. In trying to objectify that Absolute, he can only call
up the closed and empty space where he meets death: the Ice
Church. Peer Gynt, whose imaginative avoidance of all commitment was no less central to Ibsen's genius, is the other side
of the same false coin. His is the trolls' motto: "To yourself
be—enough!" What happens? Abducting and abandoning the
bride Ingrid, begetting and disowning a bastard troll-child,
leaving Solveig eternally waiting in the doorway as he goes
"roundabout," Peer too refuses all genuine mutuality. He must
be always on the move toward a demonic freedom that is elsewhere. And in trying to objectify his own histrionic evasions,
he can only call up a series of increasingly prison-like scenarios
within an empty openness—from the trolls' cave to the desert
and the crossroads. Each play, however, leads us beyond its
mask of the suicidal will—beyond its protagonist who ironically closes himself within the world called up by his self-
absenting desire to possess—toward the symbolic affirmation
of a counter-truth. *Brand* leads us beyond the heroic self-de-
ceptions of its pseudo-Kierkegaard to a final question: "If
not by Will," Brand cries, "how can Man be redeemed?"
And a voice out of the thunderous avalanche proclaims:
"He is the God of Love." *Peer Gynt* leads us beyond the

heroic nothingness of its virtuoso role-player to a comple-
mentary question: "Where was my self," cries Peer, "my whole
self, my true self?" The answer here comes from the abandoned
bride and mother, Solveig "In my faith, in my hope, in my
love." But neither play can show within the performed action
the meaning of its mysterious concluding pronouncement. The
criticism of the will, here as elsewhere in Ibsen, remains cru-
cially negative.

—*But what has that negative criticism to do with Ibsen's
later realism?*

—Ibsen said that he could just as easily have made Brand
a sculptor or a politician. And he was right: whatever its
ostensible subject, a major Ibsen play always renders our attempt to grasp and possess in "freedom" some imagined absolute. And it always implies an ironic criticism of that self-de-
luded attempt. As Ibsen approached "realism"—as he shaped
his style to accord more closely with the system of forms that
is called into being by our will to know and possess the object
—he continued to ask: Why do we idealists, artists, and seek-
ers of new life find that our action turns on itself and becomes
its own negation? And he honestly and ironically mimed the
processes by which we shut ourselves into our secular equivalents of the Ice Church. But within the "realistic" world of objective surfaces no one can hear a final voice out of the
thunder or put riddles to a symbolic Solveig. As an inclusive
symbolic form, "realism" brings into focus an existence within
which religious symbols have lost all authenticity. When the
"realistic" texture assumes symbolic point, it can manifest no
more than the absence of death that has resulted from our
desire to possess the world-as-object. That death now tends
to appear as the meaning of both the protagonist's action and
the play's own style. And we can now move beyond that double
self-closure within the surfaces of an objectified and alienated
world only by participating in the field of play that we meet
in performance.

—*You take those Norwegian drawing-rooms, and the box-
stage itself, finally to be Ibsen's images of that self-closure?*

—So they became, in the course of his theatrical exploration.

And Ingmar Bergman is still using their film equivalents for rather similar purposes.

—*Then how does the ending of* A Doll's House *fit your account? After surviving her tarantella, her purgative dance of death, Nora breaks out of this bourgeois enclosure.*

—But where can she go? Her slamming of that door raises as many questions as the voice in Brand's avalanche. Can such a histrionic protagonist really move beyond the social scenarios, the whole array of dolls' houses, that will tempt her to become a dancing puppet? The "optimism" of this play, as Hermann Weigand argued years ago, is ironic indeed. Do we want to follow Nora "elsewhere," as we follow Brand and Peer Gynt? Well, Ibsen does something very much like that in the plays to come. Does the ostensibly self-liberating Mrs. Alving in *Ghosts* open her haunted house at all? No. She chooses to close it more tightly.

—*Chooses? But surely Maurice Valency has made the obvious point: "Like Oedipus, he said, "she has no more choices or decisions to make. She has only to wait for the revelation to be made, and the blow to fall."*

—That's true of neither Oedipus nor Mrs. Alving. Though historical circumstances can't be undone, nothing has determined the detailed movement of the present action. Tempted by an abstract and self-deceptive idealism, Mrs. Alving wants both to be free of the past and to substantiate her empty vision of the future by possessing her son Oswald. We can see that most clearly in Act 3, where mother and son try to dominate each other in the name of freedom. There we act and witness a double self-closure that neither character wants to understand. Like Rosmersholm, the Alving drawing-room perpetuates its own ghosts.

—*And you think the contrast between that claustral room and the glacial mountainscape outside the Alving window makes a comment not only upon the characters' self-entrapment but also upon the play's realistic style?*

—As so often in Ibsen's plays, we see two forms of a single death: feverish self-closure within a possessed world and icy self-exclusion from the possibilities of life. But not until *The*

Wild Duck, I suspect, does Ibsen's "realism" find itself directly mirrored or at least parodied in its own images of closure and exclusion. The Ekdal flat is there a "realistic" stage-within-the-stage, where a histrionic family can be spied upon and manipulated by a neurotic young man who thinks he seeks truth. (And the Ekdal loft, of course, is a "romantic" stage-within-the-stage-within-the-stage, a "briny deep" where the darker meanings of the action can assume symbolic point.) The performed action in *The Wild Duck* leaves us with an impossible choice between Dr. Relling's defensive life-lies and Gregers Werle's yet more defensive exposure of such lies—a choice between a stage-full of mediocre Peer Gynts and a mediocre Brand who'd like to be both playwright and audience. The dilemma is characteristic of Ibsen's negative criticism of the will—which here reaches out to provide a wry image of our theatrical event itself. But the image is necessarily incomplete. The action of performance, by inviting us to find the masks of Relling, Gregers, and the Ekdals (to say nothing of Haakon Werle and Mrs. Sörby) among us and within us, leads us past that dilemma. We move beyond both the life-lie and its exposure through a participatory witnessing that the performed action can't directly render.

Then in *Rosmersholm*—which Valency, by the way, thinks is "essentially expository"—Ibsen brings into focus yet more faithfully detailed analogies between the performed action and the "realistic" dimension of the action of performance. The result, as I've indicated, is a masterly critique of the objectifying will —in the artistic terms that have been posited by that will itself.

—*If so, why doesn't Ibsen let* Hedda Gabler *then move beyond realism?*

—One step at a time. That play does move toward the enigmatic involution of the later Ibsen. It rebuffs our analytic efforts even while inviting us further into the cold and closed space that Hedda inhabits. We may speculate endlessly on the exact nature of her motives according to some "realistic" psychology: there's an excess of possible causes. But it's clear that she tries to become both playwright and audience as she maneuvers others toward a "beauty" that embodies her secret desire for death. And like Rebecca West, when trapped in circumstances arising from her avoidance of mutuality, she withdraws to a position that mirrors our own: behind the curtains opposite our fourth wall. We hear her frenzied interior music. She calls out, "I can hear what you're saying, Tesman." And when the pistol-shot sounds from that cell of listening absence, doesn't the play coldly convict us? Hedda is for us what Løvborg has been for her. We too have been vicariously enjoying a projected death-in-life. Judge Brack, our ironic chorus, fends off co-responsibility by trying to see Hedda's death as a mere spectacle in the next curtained box: "But, good God! People don't do such things!" We do. With that shot, Ibsen's "realism" has cancelled itself. From now on, the performed action will no longer tempt the self-deceived voyeur. It will occur within our shared awareness that, as negated self-negations, we are speeding toward Absence.

—*That sounds more like Genet or Beckett than Ibsen.*

—The later Ibsen is more like Genet or Beckett than the texture of his prose might suggest. By 1890 Ibsen had reached the transitional point that Mallarmé saw in Shakespeare's *Hamlet*—which he called "halfway between the old multiple-action method and the Monologue, the drama of the self, which belongs to the future." In *The Master Builder* the ambiguous symptoms of self-closure—Solness' arrogance, his sense of empty accomplishment, his fear of the younger generation, his wife's mousey frustration, her inability to nourish children, the puzzlingly contradictory stories offered by this couple—have become signs of a demonic predicament that seems to shape the action, from the mysterious fire to Hilde's opportune knocking at the door. It is significant that for Solness the account offered by Hilde of the "forgotten" past—his kiss, his fairy-tale promise—will need no verifying: if he has not done what she alleges, he "should have done it." As Hofmannsthal was to say in *The Book of Friends*, "All fantasy in which you intensely participate is myth." And Solness chooses with Hilde to *live* this myth of using the world to build or possess the highest tower. The consequences, as here unfolded, include the transformation of our field of play into a humanly empty dream of vertiginous ecstasy. *The Master Builder* invites us also to enter the myth and experience that transformation. We don't simply observe the mutual hypnotism of Solness and Hilde from the "outside." The play's gradually shifting style enables it to move beyond the ostensible "realism" in which it begins toward just such a lucid dream-action as the protagonists themselves are living. When we listen to what Maeterlinck called Solness' and Hilde's tacit dialogue of the "second degree," or when we gaze at Hilde gazing ecstatically at that invisible image atop the tower from which Solness has already fallen, a gestural poetry leads us to participate directly in this dream. We too apprehend the performed action as an image of our ominously gratifying power to reduce every "other" to the status of a magical sign of our condition. No wonder this play has been read as autobiographical allegory. Part of what such a reading misses is the way in which a performance asks us to share Ibsen's experience of desolating and finally impotent power.

By the end of a yet later play, *John Gabriel Borkman*, when Ella Rentheim and Mrs. Borkman ("We two shadows—over the dead man") clasp hands in a cold void that is symbolically identical with the Borkman closed room, the performed action has become a double image of self-exclusion and self-enclosure. And the dialogue between the characters—which seems to speak also of our shadowy presences in the theater itself—has become a recognition of our commitment to a death-producing shared monologue. It's only a step further to a real "drama of the Self"—the "epilogue" of the series that began with *A Doll's House*. In the stylized world of *When We Dead Awaken*, setting and characters correspond to the obsessively selective vision of the protagonist—the artist Rubek who had once sculpted an array of sardonic "portrait busts" with "animal faces behind the masks." Ibsen's "realism" has now become one retrospective item in a more inclusive self-reflection. As we gaze with Ibsen upon Rubek, we also gaze with Rubek upon a mirror constructed in stone, "a man weighed down by guilt." "I call him remorse—remorse for a forfeited life," he says. "He sits there and dips his fingers in the rippling water—to wash them clean; and he is gnawed and tormented by the knowledge that he will never, never succeed. He will never, in all eternity, free himself, and be granted resurrection. He must stay for ever in his Hell." With Ibsen and Rubek we share the narcissist's self-confirming vision of his "fate." Ever since *Brand*, in fact, we have been doubly miming that hell of remorse from which no mask of the will can free itself.

—*But* When We Dead Awaken *does move toward new life.*

—There is talk of new life. Rubek and his Irene do climb, like a glacially gay Rosmer and Rebecca, toward their marriage in the icy whiteness. But Brand's avalanche overwhelms them. As the rigid Sister of Mercy shrieks, the triumphant song of the huntress Maia rises from below. That counterpoint between the self-closed *personae* of spirit and nature is Ibsen's last acknowledgment that he could dramatize only through negation the realm indicated by the voice out of the thunder. Only by calling us to share the closed spaces of his protagonists could he implicitly move beyond the chosen fate of those preachers, actors, and artists who—as Hofmannsthal once put it—are "silent mirrors in which one recognizes oneself." And only through our participation, which opens us to the characters and each other in a way that would be impossible for Rubeck, does the title of *When We Dead Awaken* go beyond irony. As in *Rosmersholm*, so throughout Ibsen's career.

—*Perhaps. But to demonstrate that these plays confirm the intention you find in* Rosmersholm, *you'd need a series of full-scale analyses—each of which would no doubt seem to me quite reductive.*

—Doesn't analysis always reduce to a simplified replica, on the basis of the chosen analytical principles? The question is: does my analysis point to an important pattern in our playing? But I must confess that, on my own grounds, the case is far from complete. Though I tried to lay out the present action of *Rosmersholm*, I hardly touched upon the moment-by-moment relations among characters, actors, and witnesses that constitute the life of our playing. *Rosmersholm* judges me as it does Freud: I've remained outside the play, talking about an objectified construct.

—*Where else could you be? As critics, aren't we essentially external and analytic observers?*

—Loveless masks of the will? Trying, like Rosmer or Rebecca, to master a field of play from which we thereby exclude ourselves? If so, some Ibsenite demiurge is our playwright, and our conversation is itself a closed space, a hell . . . .

—*From which, in all eternity, you can't hope to free yourself. You're trapped by your own interpretation.*

—Then there's only one way out. We must leave Ibsen. Take the Button Molder's advice.

—*Kill ourselves? Not me.*

—Or wake from the dead. Disappear, along with our objectified worlds.

—*That's hardly a subject for drama, and no basis at all for criticism.*

—"On the contrary," as the dying Ibsen is said to have said. It became Strindberg's great subject after his Inferno-crisis, and whether it's a basis for criticism must be for us an open question. Can we let our habitually objectifying voices be still? Can we listen to a critical fiction that might enter into the play's action of performance? If so . . .

—*Yes?*

— . . . maybe *The Ghost Sonata* can begin.

FOUR

SEEING THE
HIDDEN

2 November 1972:

A play of the dead. Music. But find the action. Or does this script haunt me only because I can't grasp it? Stupid, then, to imagine a production.

Was Dürrenmatt right? "Modern drama has come out of Strindberg: we have never gone beyond the second scene of *The Ghost Sonata.*" A strong scene, yes: Hummel at the ghost supper. Climax: a mutual exposure of the hidden, a stopping of time. Hummel shrivels. In that moment the play grasps *us.* But how can an audience be expected to follow the exposition in Scene 1? And that talky Scene 3 seems to lie flat on the page. Give it up? Or risk hanging myself with my own rope?

3 November:

The critics aren't much help. Martin Lamm: "Despite the limitations implied in its chamber music title, *The Ghost Sonata* exceeds the possibilities of stage presentation in its attempt to depict simultaneously how people can show one personality to the world and live another within themselves." Mood: "black misanthropy." (Shall we do Pirandello instead?) Eric Bentley: a dialectic in three scenes—statement, counterstatement, conclusion. But the weak ending indicates Strindberg's "failure to find a meaning in life which he could confirm from inner experience. His religion is always pasted on." (Shall we do Brecht?) Maurice Valency: "many faults"—story too complex, incoherent, hyperbolic. But "extraordinary efficacy as drama, in spite of its obvious puerility from an intellectual viewpoint." (Let's settle for Tennessee Williams.)

6 November:

Good—Evert Sprinchorn hears a music in three movements: allegro, largo, andante. Explore those motifs he mentions: *Die Walküre*, *Faust*, windows, vampirism, sleepwalking. The style of playing must realize that music. But what's the action? To penetrate the house?

Or is this a Freudian dreamwork? Robert Corrigan thinks that the Student dreams the play: "a series of images progressing in such a way as to reveal their coherent importance to Arkenholz." But if so, why isn't the Student more consistently central? Why let Hummel steal the show in Scene 2? (Or is that exactly Hummel's objective: to steal the show?) And why begin with that scrubbed and sunny realism—almost a Swedish Vermeer? This is entirely different from *A Dream Play* where the sets—as Strindberg told August Falck—might well suggest Turner. Only in Scene 2 do we arrive at Edward Munch. And then we move on toward Böcklin. A deepening dream? Or life *into* dream?

7 November:

Landslide. So today the voters have requested four more glorious years. "Peace is at hand," says our Metternich—even though the 31 October agreement was never signed. Over six million Vietnamese now killed, wounded, or made homeless. Our nearly four million tons of bombs *must* have saved them. The Buddha was right: "This house is on fire." We're a nation of sleepwalking killers.

Like Hummel? He wants to expose the crimes, settle the accounts, install the two innocents in the house—for a new life. He can't see the drowned Milkmaid at first because he won't Scenes 1 and 2: Hummel's self-deceptive action. (Mephisto plays God.) Scenes 1 and 3: Arkenholz's temptation and ordeal. (Parzival learns that he isn't Siegfried? Though he thinks he has saved people from a collapsing house, he now wants to possess this one. He too is burning.) Two interlocked dreampaths?

Midnight. After the hoked-up urgency of the network commentators, I find in these old *TDR* pages a relatively sane voice: Artaud's notes for a production of *The Ghost Sonata*. "We have lived and dreamed everything this play reveals, but we have forgotten." Yes—and isn't this play *our* dream, within which Arkenholz and Hummel dream their own lives? Artaud wants to assault us with this nightmare. Shatter our frozen violence with an eruption of truth. Noise, light, distorted perspectives. For him the peaceful ending is a fault, but one that might "clarify the play for that part of the audience who is afraid of the unconscious."

And yet, doesn't Artaud's violence destroy the subtler music of this script? Better to follow its own clues to tempo and design. Visually, a self-transforming world—from pseudo-Vermeer to Munch to Böcklin. Let the performance lead us (as the action leads the characters: magically) from those deceptively peaceful suburban surfaces through an inner violence that is eating itself, smothering itself, toward . . . what? This is no individual Freudian dream but our shared dream-work: life as a self-elucidating dream that moves toward . . . waking. And just as "life" is here deathly, so Böcklin's "Isle of the Dead" must finally point toward true life—the peace that is at hand if we relax our spastic grip on objects, stop trying to possess what can only be the appearances of our dream-play. That's the hidden end, the *telos* of our dream. Not at all pasted on. Spine: to disclose the hidden? to end time?

7 December:

Sunday afternoon, exactly thirty-one years ago today, a rehearsal of *The Messiah*: then coming out into the peaceful twilit street, "Alleluia!" ringing in our ears—and hearing "Extra! Extra!" The old counterpoint?

Perhaps we could try it this way: Curtain opens on a sunny Stockholm square. Strong yellows. Echoing and answering forms. Blinds drawn in the Round Room. Blue, white, pink hyacinths in the next window. A blue spread and two white pillowcases on the balcony railing above. White sheets over the second-story windows. (Hidden life. What youth, marriage, death within?) A woman in black, motionless in the doorway. A window-mirror. (What hidden life, or death, watching?) Later, when the blinds are raised in the Round Room, we'll see a sunlit marble statue of a young woman, surrounded by palms. (Life? Death?) In front of the house the Caretaker's Wife sweeping, polishing, watering. (Rhythmic, absorbed, quietly compulsive.) Tubbed laurels. A green bench. Downstage right —an area to be associated with the Student's temptation—an advertising pillar, a telephone booth. Near-by in a wheelchair, the Old Man with white beard and spectacles is avidly reading a newspaper and occasionally glancing at the house. Downstage left—an area that may become associated with innocence and vision—a quiet fountain.

The set is a bright façade, apparently solid. Not like Teo Otto's set for the Steckel production of 1952 in Zurich, where expressionistic distortions located the audience at once in a dream: tilted fountain and pillar; angled flats as side-street houses; the Round Room itself out of line, potentially translucent. No. This suburban square must seem a brightly objective world that we might spy upon, grasp, possess. (Hummel is already doing just that.) We must be tempted by the illusion of realism, which offers us just such a world. And yet, this *could* be the world of a fairy-tale. The composed surfaces and silent actions lead eyes and mind toward unknown interiors, receding perspectives, hidden meanings. Church bells peal in the distance. A Sunday pause. Then a Milkmaid enters to refresh herself at the fountain, her ordinary gestures completing the scene. No dialogue. We are to keep our eyes open. Organ notes drift in. A steamship bell. What sea voyage is beginning?

When the Student enters, unshaven, unrested, and crosses to the fountain, that's the first dissonant note. (He's at once included in the Old Man's glances.) Then as he asks the Milkmaid for the cup, we can see her terror. Amid this freshness, something sinister. And then, just as suddenly, we're struck by the Old Man's amazement: "Who's he talking to? I can't see anyone. Is he mad?" Is the uncanny intruder then not the Student but the Milkmaid? But if so, what about the Student—and ourselves? With what clairvoyance have we already begun to see past those bright surfaces? We find ourselves cooperating with a visionary action that is already moving through us.

That's crucial. The action—"to disclose the hidden"—must shape not only the setting, characters, and dialogue, but also the moment-by-moment participation of witnesses and actors. Together we will penetrate these sunlit façades, enter a dark and fantastic interior, and move toward a simple light that shines in the darkness. Scene 1 leads us past the Sunday order into a monstrous disorder—hinted at in the Milkmaid's terror and then in Hummel's talk about the residents, his own chilling grip upon the Student's hand, and his later fear of the Milkmaid (during that grotesque theophany when beggars draw him in his wheelchair like some Thor). Within the Round Room, Scene 2 unfolds that disorder and leads us toward a transcendent order. Bengtsson shows Johansson the Mummy hidden in the closet—and tells of the Daughter's sickness. Then the Mummy comes out to haunt Hummel, her former lover, and warn him away from their Daughter. Then Hummel strips the masks from the Mummy's husband, the Colonel, and proceeds—after the arrival of his former Fiancée (once seduced by the Colonel, now crazy) and the Baron (once also the Mummy's lover, now perhaps a jewel-thief)—to announce retribution. But then the peripety: stopping the clock of judgment, the Mummy unmasks Hummel and sends him into the closet to hang himself. For some time the Student has been visible in the Hyacinth Room, almost as an oblique witness, but now a light comes up on the Daughter, too, with her harp. A prelude, and the Student sings:

> I saw the sun.
> I seemed to see the Hidden One.

It's a precarious moment, suggesting not only the irony of blind innocence amid corruption but also the possibility of an innocence *beyond* corruption. On that ambiguous note: curtain. And the troublesome Scene 3 will have to engage the ambiguity. But how? Try tomorrow to work towards an answer by setting

down in detail how we all—characters, witnesses, actors—
share the action. Sleep on it.

8 December:

First, how do the characters "disclose the hidden?" For those
who want to be grounded only in themselves, "to penetrate,"
"to expose," and "to see" are ways of possessing the object.
Hummel expands from a reader of the news to a nightmare
image of voyeur, tempter, landlord, judge, vampire. His "inter-
minably long life" is "a book of fairy-tales" with a recurrent
leitmotif. His subtlety is rooted in the gross vampirism that we
see more directly in the spying Cook of Scene 3, herself a
Hummel. And the vigor of this crippled Jacob re-appears in
the neurotically absorptive frailty of the Daughter. Symbolic
details focus him as Mephisto, Thor, Wotan, a worn-out Don
Juan, an unforgiving Jehovah, or the Old Adam. He seems related to everyone—by blood, secret liaisons, echoes and con-
tinuations, transformations. Hummel and Mummy, Hummel and
Bengtsson: reversible pairs, like Pozzo and Lucky in *Waiting for
Godot.* In short, we know Hummel as we know ourselves. He's
the Prince of this World, and the old stock from which we have
sprung. (His most recent reincarnation? Dr. Abrahamson, the
prying and guilty judge-advocate of Ingmar Bergman's *Rite*—
a character who mirrors the film's spectators.)

Hummel's way of action, disguised as romance or morality,
can seduce the Student (and us) in the Faustian temptation of
Scene 1 and give us a deceptive sense of finality in the retribution of Scene 2. But his way also contains a defensive counter-
action: "to hide," "to refuse to see," "to be blind." Hummel
himself is a master of evasion; the Fiancée looks out on the
world through her window-mirror; the Mummy buries herself
in the closet. A theme amplified in images of screens, eyes,
windows—including (see Sprinchorn's translation) Hummel's
remark on the Student's pronunciation of "window," a word
that he hasn't uttered. Both action and counter-action drive toward an exposure of their own inner death—cold, mummifica-
tion, atrophy, bloating, cancer. Hence the climax of Scene 2.

On this level *The Ghost Sonata* enacts Strindberg's nightmare vision of Ibsen's great subject: the self-contradiction of ego-life. The will, said Schopenhauer, "buries its teeth in its own flesh." (Dorothy, who has been re-reading *The Father*, said at breakfast this morning: "That play is a battle between a two-headed beast that is eating itself.") The apparent end of this plot in Scene 2 is no incoherence but part of the play's pattern of tempting disclosures. If we understood what Hummel means, who he *is*, we would know that he must continue to live his death in Scene 3—in the Daughter, the Cook, and Arkenholz himself. But we're tempted to imagine that he can be eliminated from a world which otherwise remains the same. We underestimate the difficulty of the Student's implicit quest.

What is that quest? For those who don't demand absolute self-determination, "to see the hidden" means a way of visionary understanding and purgation. This way begins for the Student with his second-sight as a "Sunday child," which he accepts and uses (as we do) before knowing its implications. But he is in conflict between this way of action and Hummel's— and he's only half-prepared to see himself. His encounter with the Milkmaid is a distorted action of refreshing, healing, and opening the eyes: it's the ironic beginning of the "trial" he has earned through saving people from that collapsing house—as all self-conscious and therefore blinding "virtue" earns its trials. Dazed, naive, he's now tempted to possess this house and its hyacinthine young lady. But this house is in fact the collapsing house which he *is*—and from which he must be saved. A grail quester who'd like to be a conquering prince, an incipient Christ who makes a Faustian pact, he imagines a romantic shortcut to the transcendental. He therefore involves himself in a possessive seeing, a refusal to see his own involvement, and finally (in Scene 3) a violent exposure of the hidden that echoes those made by Hummel, the Mummy, and his own father. An ambivalent son, he has been tempted to become a Hummel—and he does "murder" the Daughter with his truth—but his potential nature is that Arkenholz or "saving wood" which can transcend the flood of time and space or the ego-world.

This second way of disclosing the hidden is also dynamic—

relaxing the impulse to cling, allowing the death of that possessive spy who is "me," and so moving toward a pure beholding. (Toward that luminous "show" that Hummel wants to "steal!") In the Student, lust for the object modulates toward a compassionate attention to the other *dramatis personae*—visionary forms who image his own complex identity. On this level *The Ghost Sonata* enacts a grail ordeal, a stage in the purgation of ego-life, which points to a "death" beyond Hummel's. The Student's nearly final request is for "patience in our time of trial" and "purity of will." (His final request is not for himself but for the Daughter.) And since the world presented by the play *is* his purgatory, the transcendence of ego-life must be imaged as a limit-situation—a dissolving of time and place, a waking from the dream of this world. A waking to Böcklin's vision of the end of our sea-voyage.

Scene by scene, then—the performed action: In Scene 1 Hummel engages in an oblique spying-exposing-and-hiding through which he tries to gain possession of Arkenholz, the Sunday child. For Hummel wants above all to possess what he refuses to become. The Student's action consists of more ambiguously hesitant, delightedly confused maneuvers, half-consciously designed to gain entry into the house without facing the implications of doing so. We can outline each "beat" in those terms. Hummel's flattering approach arouses the Student's engagingly modest pride. When he then introduces himself as an old acquaintance, the Student (as expected) coldly withdraws. But when Hummel then comes on as a crippled helper, a victim of ingratitude who himself now needs a bit of help, the Student finds himself pushing the wheelchair. And when Hummel offers a job that begins with a visit to the opera, the Student is happy to take it. From then on, Hummel plays upon an aroused curiosity—the "exposition" is under way—until he risks demonstrating his chill grip. The Student panics at that, but he's prevented from escaping by the spectacle of the Daughter. A devil's bargain? No, a gift, an inheritance! The Student is hooked. Though the ominous vision of the Dead Man and Johansson's yet more ominous sketch of Hummel will suggest again to the Student that he'd better get out while he can, the

Daughter has only to drop her bracelet and he's back on the hook. From then on, he can do no more than anxiously rationalize his capture: *he* doesn't like to be ungrateful. And when Hummel-Thor hails him as a Sunday hero, won't he glow in gratified embarrassment?

Scene 2 expands for us some of the implications that the Student is refusing to face. Now several characters engage in the spying-exposing-and-hiding, through a series of increasingly tense encounters (Johansson disclosing the Mummy, the Mummy surprising Hummel, Hummel stripping the Colonel), an ironically gracious interlude (as the naive but disingenuous Student enters), and the ghost supper. In this scene each act of possessive exposure alerts us to a history of such acts and sets the stage for yet another—until the repentant but vindictive Mummy's judgment *seems* to bring the murderous chain to a moral conclusion. Then the Student's song invites us further inward, to join him in the Hyacinth Room. But it also points beyond his present understanding. Like his role as savior, his Sunday vision, and the hyacinths themselves, the song is a sign. Only at his peril does he think to possess such signs.

Scene 3 makes that clear. The opening reverie shared by Student and Daughter seems idyllic romance, but it is really a love feast of the self-deceptive mutual possession that tries to grasp in time the images that point beyond time. The Daughter may know this. Are they ready to wed? "Not yet," she says. What remains? "The waiting, the trials, the patience." That remark introduces the next unit of dialogue—her exposure of the hidden as another test for the Student. The third and final unit begins with the Student's question: "Do you love honesty?" Now *he* exposes the hidden as another test for *her*. Both exposures are partly defensive and vampire-like; both ordeals are earned by those who suffer them. As the play's karma works itself out, the Daughter dies and the Student moves beyond his violence in a moment of cathartic self-recognition. Entering a mood of benediction, he again sings "The Song of the Sun"— now accompanied by magical harp and white light, and now pointing to the play's final vision.

But if the entire performed action is *our* dream, how do we who witness or dream it engage in "disclosing the hidden?" It's clear that the full music of this play locates us within the Student's conflict. We too have the Sunday child's vision. For us too the play is a visionary opening into a life in which we participate. But, like him, we also want to be romantic voyeurs. Our proscenium window is like the Fiancée's window-mirror that gives news of a life from which she ineffectively hides. That's why we are tempted at the outset by realism: this style renders exactly that temptation we all experience when, as sleepwalkers in life, we think ourselves closed subjects in a world of objects. At first, like the Student, we are dazed, bewildered by complexities we haven't quite grasped, in a world that seems real. It *is* "real"; it is the "world." It's not the product of a private unconscious in contrast to "real waking life," but precisely "real waking life" that will soon reveal its hidden nature as dream. For the play assumes that we do dream our lives, that we experience a purgatorial world through shared mediating projections, and that waking from this world is "death" to the ego-consciousness.

In effect, the play urges us to remember the burden of the Tibetan text that has lately been running in my mind: "For one of ordinary intellect, the best religious practice is to regard all objective things as though they were images seen in a dream or produced by magic." Why? Because life so regarded contains its own movement toward detachment. Strindberg had apparently found a related teaching in Swedenborg. When a man is born again—according to this teaching—his desires aren't stripped away at once "for that would be equivalent to destroying the whole man." So "for a long while evil spirits are left with him, to stir up his desires that they may be dissolved in many ways." (*Zones of the Spirit.*) Surely that describes the purgatorial dream-world of this play. As its original title indicates, it takes place in *kama-loka*. But this *kama-loka* isn't just post-mortem: it mirrors our present existence. Ghosts? In his novel *Black Banners*, Strindberg says that "ghosts" are "apparent images of living or dead persons." All the characters in *The Ghost Sonata* are ghosts, for each other and for us. Our entire field of play consists of *appearances* that speak to our condition. We mime here what Strindberg in *The Blue Book* called "the somnambulism and clairvoyance of everyday life."

Because the play is not a private dream (any more than the Milkmaid is merely a private apparition for Hummel within the play) the Student's vision and ours can be analogous and convergent. In Scene 1 we share his increasing sense of the dreamlike quality of the action. Its coincidences, from the initial meeting with Hummel on through the Daughter's dropping of the bracelet, are tacit signs. Its swift flow and its strange harmonies constitute a hidden invitation. We are participating in a medium that reflects us, answers us, leads us. We must follow this music. In Scene 2 we seem to overtake the Student by remaining in the Round Room with the ghost supper. But then his song seems to leap ahead of that music of corruption. Catching up with him in Scene 3, we make the dreamlike discovery that some time has already elapsed and that he looks back on Scene 2 as we do but with fuller knowledge. Then, as he elucidates the action, we join him in seeing how those who want to possess this house *are* the house in its deathliness.

What then? "When you've seen yourself, you die," says the Stranger in *The Burned House*. In *The Ghost Sonata* the house itself disappears. The action dissolves. Light only on the singing Arkenholz, as we realize that we have dreamed a shared dream—shaped to disclose our hidden identity, pointed toward the transcendence of ego-action in a pure beholding. We realize what the Teacher in Strindberg's fragmentary continuation, *The Isle of the Dead*, will merely *say**: "if life is a dream,

---

* *13 April 1973*:

Merely *say*? But when writing that, I hadn't witnessed René Farabet's remarkably stylized playing of the Teacher in Henri Ronse's production for the Théâtre Oblique—which brought more life to *The Isle of the Dead* at the Petit Odéon last night than I'd thought possible. Farabet's precisely modulated gestures, bodily and vocal, suggested some acerbic transcendental music—a Nō play for the occident. (And as the play-within-the-play, *The Stronger* was a Beardsley print in motion, offering a mordant perspective on the "living.") Ronse's principles—spelled out in *Obliques 1* and also informing his production of *The Pelican*—would lead to an exciting *Ghost Sonata* quite different from mine: a play stripped

then the play is a dream about a dream," and both kinds of dream are "instructive." Now we no longer focus our alter-ego, who has lost himself in a moment of compassion. Darkness. Stage-time ends. And now, no longer partly a window-mirror on an objectified world we think to possess, our visionary aperture reflects an arrival after our dream-voyage: Böcklin's "Isle of the Dead"—a small boat approaching those craggy shores of darkness and light. (Projected onto an invisible scrim?) Then we wake from our shared dream of a shared dream.

Finally, how do those who act—including the witnesses as implicit actors—"disclose the hidden?" That's what we must find in rehearsal. Don't clutter the mind in advance. But do note that our playing-style must itself lead us from life into dream—by gradually externalizing the dream that has been informing the life. It must proceed steadily from the clean (and slightly fairy-tale) realism with which Scene 1 opens, through the grotesquely choreographed rigidity (carapaced and shriveling figures out of Munch) that Scene 2 demands, into the hot-house lyricism (bloated etiolated figures) of Scene 3. Each actor must find in himself and increasingly manifest the Hummel violence that is blinding, suffocating, and eating itself. Can we generate a pattern of "contagicus" behavior—gestures embodying the desire to see and not be seen, the struggle to breathe, the pangs of hunger? By Scene 3, at least, the sexuality of such a pattern of slow-motion tics must be clear. Nothing so blatant as Bergman's notion of having the Student finally dive for the Daughter's pudenda. But the symbol of uterine cancer, which lurks behind this script, must somehow be there. Arms: warding off, reaching out for help, grasping. Points of focus: eyes, throat, solar plexus, groin.

Note also one paradox: we can open up this apparently pessimistic action only as we find in our present playing, some-

of all "realistic" and "psychological" representation in order to disclose the "latent theatricality" of the text, its "ghost of a theater of the unconscious." The images of melodrama, within a constantly modulated chiaroscuro lighting, would constitute a hauntingly symbolic nightmare. "The light," Ronse says, "must *invent* the actor."

thing of that joy or energy-filled peace to which the Student hasn't yet awakened. Mere anguish or misanthropy would block us. And the intensity that unfolds for us in rehearsal must surely be the present end of our playing? Though the performed action seems to move through purgatorial time toward a transcendent end, our action of performance must disclose that end as among us now. There is no peace in the world—but peace is at hand. A contradiction? No: the most important secret of this play *as* a play. And Strindberg must have known that it is exactly the secret of Eastern non-dualism. Approached as "reality," Māyā reveals itself to be a purgatorial illusion from which the Student may find deliverance. But rightly understood, Māyā is also Līlā—a cosmic "playing" within which we glimpse the shared presence that is our ground and goal. "We should act in the world," said Ramana Maharshi, "as an actor does on the stage. In all actions there subsists the background of the real 'I,' which is the underlying principle." That real "I," the only Actor, is what the *Bhagavad-Gita* calls the "Witness," the one Knower of the field, the single sun that illuminates the world. Remember, too, that mantra from the *Upanishads*: "He who is in the Sun is also in you."

> I saw the Sun.
> I seemed to see the Hidden One.

Yes—and if the Student doesn't realize the most deeply hidden meaning of his song, our action of performance must do so.

Something of this must have been present for Rilke when he attended in 1915 the Munich Hoftheater's production of what he called this "truly incredible" play. "At first it seems too hopelessly obstinate to present humanity's disconsolation as its absolute condition," he said, "but when someone like this has power over even the most disconsolate, there hovers above the whole, unspoken, a concept of illimitable human greatness. And a desperate love." This play, along with *The Dance of Death*, had "almost reconciled" him to the theater—"which for years has given me nothing."

But cast it right after Christmas. Then we'll see.

23 December:

It is rumored that Nixon consulted neither the Joint Chiefs of Staff nor the Security Council before starting this past week's bombing of Hanoi and Haiphong. In America we seem stunned or indifferent. The London *Guardian*: "Are we to conclude that the American President, who commands a nuclear force now capable of destroying all human life, is not responsive to advice? The question is a dreadful one to ask but it will have to be asked." And even Senator Saxbe has decided that Nixon "must be out of his mind." No. However magnified in scale, this is the normal action of the mind that says: "I believe in the battle." Nixon's mind, our mind, Hummel's mind. That's why at the outset Hummel must not appear sinister. Establish his paternal benevolence, his tone of right-thinking. Even in Scene 2 he believes that he can abolish crime and set up his Daughter and the Student as bourgeois householders. We too must believe it—despite the gathering nightmare.

Write out notes on all the characters—then tear them up. Each of us must find his own spine within our action. And must I then play Hummel, whom I recognize as my own mistaken identity? From *The Blue Book*: "You know yourself that when one awakes from somnambulism, one finds the world quite mad."

20 January 1973:

After too many bumbling rehearsals, we're in motion. At one point something like this:

HUMMEL (*cringing in terror as the drowning Milkmaid fixes her gaze on him*): Johansson, take me away! Quickly! Arkenholz, don't forget *The Valkyrie*!

ARKENHOLZ (*jamming Hummel's line*): What does all this mean?

JOHANSSON (*almost simultaneously, as he wheels off Hummel*): We shall see. We shall see.

"All right, no break. Right into Scene 2. Props for the Round Room! Keep up the speed."

"What a crazy race-through. But we were getting into something this time."

"As if going faster than you can think helps to find the action?"

"You felt it? When she dropped her bracelet, you said 'Look!' even before it hit the ground."

"And before I could speak, you were turning to look."

"No action and reaction but—"

"—almost dreaming it together. And from then on—"

"—we were in it."

"Letting *it* dream *you*. Stay with that feeling of synchronized action, even when we slow down again. It's everywhere. Remember how, just as the sky clouds over and my Fiancée shuts her mirror-window, the Dead Man comes out of the door in his winding-sheet? And just a moment ago, how the Milkmaid began to drown as I talked of saving her? This *is* an inauguration—no? Bengtsson, Johansson—quickly!"

24 January:

Beth's vigorous disagreement with my reading of this script is turning out, ironically enough, to be a most useful basis for her role as Mummy. From the first read-through, she has objected to my "literary" notion that we can find ourselves in each character in this shared dream. Hummel, she says, is a villain with whom the audience should feel no "empathy." When I ask how anyone could give life to such a merely negative and utterly distanced role, or to what vitality in the playing anyone else could possibly respond, she has no answer but a look of disdain. And who am I to persuade her that her extreme animus toward Hummel (and toward me?) results from her own unavowed aggression? Fortunately, such tactics would be superfluous: her very resistance has helped her to find a workable line of action. In the early moments of Scene 2 her negative fascination becomes quite clear as she stalks Hummel, frightens him, threatens him with death. From within her stylized "parrot" gestures and tones, she can't avoid gradually assuming a stance and a pace that mirror those I'm finding for Hummel. She is so insistently all that I'm *not* that she becomes my shadow. Our cut-and-thrust ("If you touch her, you shall die." "I only wish her well." "But you must spare her father. I mean, my husband—" "No!") assumes the rhythm of a grotesque dance of death. And when we reach the climax of this scene, where she "takes over," she requires almost no direction. At the end of my long speech of retribution, when I speak of the death-clock ("Do you hear what she's saying? ' 'Tis time —'tis time.' In a little while she will strike. . . . I too, can strike") and bring my crutch down hard on the table, she answers me with a dignified, almost queenly crossing to the clock. Stopping the pendulum, she begins ("*clearly and earnestly,*" as the script has it) to present herself as the antithesis of both Hummel and the death-clock. "But I can halt time. I can wipe out the past, undo what has been done." No trace now of that parrot's croak. Hardly a sign of the querulous and withdrawn old woman. Behind the grave-wrappings and the white pancake she has become again the young woman Hummel might have loved twenty years ago. "We have erred and sinned, like all mortals. We are not what we seem, for our true selves live within us, condemning our failings." Yes, the eternal woman.

But a harder note then creeps into her voice: "But that you, Jacob Hummel, sit here wearing your false name and judge us proves you are worse than us. . . . You are a robber of souls. . . ." And as she embarks upon her increasingly vigorous indictment, her penitence modulates quite spontaneously into a superb self-righteousness. Despite herself, she moves back toward the tone that my Hummel had been taking a few moments before. And after she has called in Bengtsson to give evidence against me, the reversal easily completes itself. In a gesture of condescending mastery, she puts her hand over my face: "You see yourself." She strokes my ruffled feathers: "Pretty parrot, Jacob? Jacob?" And in the parrot-tones that she has used in the first part of the scene, I answer: "Jacob's here!" And she: "Can the clock strike?" And I: "Cuc-koo, cuc-koo, cuc-koo." And she: "The clock has struck." But who has become the death-clock? For Beth, as she opens the closet door and orders me to hang myself, the Mummy is the vehicle of just retribution against a character with whom we should

feel no "empathy." But for the play, Beth gives us simultaneously that *and* an image of all that Hummel himself has
been. The audience will understand.

27 January:

7 P.M. An official truce. And we're stuck in endless repeti-
tions of Scene 3. Does it ask too much of us? Tonight it went
this way:

"Sing for my flowers!"

"Is the hyacinth your flower?"

"It is my only flower. You love the hyacinth, too?"

"Above all other flowers. I love its slim figure, which rises
erect and virginal from its roots, rests on water, and sinks its
pure, white tendrils in the colorless stream. I love its colors;
the white of snow and innocence, the honey-gold of—"

"No, you don't. Cut the gabble. I don't believe a word of it.
Are you reciting from some book on the language of flowers?
What do you really *want*, Arkenholz?"

"Want? Just to get on to the next bit, I guess. I can't justify
these lines."

"All right, hyacinth girl. Why are you asking him to say
all this?"

"I . . . I want attention. Want him to find me in the flowers.
To sing to *me* as a flower. I want his strength, too, don't I?
His life."

"You don't say it."

"Can't he read my eyes? I'd hypnotize him—but I can hardly
lift my hands to the harp. If *he* could hypnotize both of us. . . .
If we could *be* all these flowers. . . ."

"Try it. Let your eyes eat him up. You're a Hummel. But
when he says, 'We are wed,' why will you pull back?"

"Because I know it's impossible. And I want to complain.
About the dirt, the cook—*them*."

"You want the dream *and* the truth? Maybe that's why you
fill the room with dying flowers. What about you, Arkenholz?"

"I play along with her? Let her make me hypnotize her? I
want the dream, too."

"Let's hear and see that wanting. But how *can* you want the dream? Don't you see her parents there in the Round Room out of the corner of your eye?"

"I'm not thinking of them—"

"And won't you soon say that the flowers confuse you, blind you?"

"They *are* too much. In fact, *she's* too much. Maybe that's why I want to hypnotize us? I've got to master the flowers, master her."

"But when she says, 'Not yet,'—you will say, 'Good'?"

"Marriage would be a kind of smothering, a death. I've got to want her and not want her."

"And what's the feeling of that?"

"Frustration. Anger. Though I can't say it to her . . . yet. Anger at this—and at the whole fake world we're in. This dirty world where Hummel pimps for his own son, where my father gets put in a madhouse because he speaks the truth, where—"

"All right. You're not thinking about any of this. But it's there. Your arms know it when you reach out toward her—to save her from this house? to rape her? to throttle her? Your eyes know it—when they want to lose themselves in her eyes, but pull away confused, blinded. It's there under the flower-speeches, waiting to erupt. Try it again from the beginning."

"Sing for my—"

"No—wait. What's beneath the anger?"

"Beneath—? Nothing."

"There's some truth, then, in the whiteness of the flowers— or in the colorless stream?"

"I don't see it."

"When you play the anger, what else is there but anger?"

"For me? Just that awareness of being the anger. Or of being *with* the anger."

"An awareness that isn't the anger."

"Or anything else."

"And if you focus on that, what happens to the anger."

"It begins to seem fake, doesn't it? It might disappear.'

"And for you as Arkenholz, what's beneath the anger? The same nothing?"

"But Arkenholz isn't an actor."

"No? Doesn't he play the modest savior? the charming lover? the angry son? Can he think he really *is* any of that?"

"But then who is he?"

"Who are you—when you're with the anger? Maybe that's what Arkenholz is, behind what he plays, behind even the mask called Arkenholz—an awareness that leads him through this fake world to disappear?"

"He sees that in the flowers?"

"Or the light. Or the colorless stream. Why else does the white Ascalon flower on that tile stove rise from the knees of Buddha? But maybe Arkenholz doesn't know what he sees there. Maybe no one sees it but us—through him. Or maybe no one sees it—through us."

"I certainly don't."

"Never mind. But stay *with* those feelings you found under the words. Try it again from the beginning."

"Sing for my flowers."

"Is the hyacinth your flower?"

"It is my only flower. . . ."

2 February:

A few post-mortem notes:

Though the candles in the Round Room were put out several hours ago, they still hover before your eyes. After-images. Maybe performance has always had something like this strange combination of immediacy and detachment. Fresh, and yet as if foreknown. As you relate to your partners, to objects, to the audience, time almost becomes a pure present, and yet that moving *now* fulfills the destined phrase, the beat, the act. And as you discover the hidden life of the role, you seem to live free of identification with that or any role. Here and now— and nowhere. Or everywhere? For in giving yourself to the role, you find yourself in the fresh and yet foreknown gestures of the others, who are no longer merely "other." A waking dream

—but never so much as tonight, ust before you were ordered to leave the stage . . . to enter the closet and hang yourself with your own rope.

Sitting in that darkened room, a stiff circle of five—Beata, the Baron, the Mummy, the Colonel, and you—eyes meeting over the candles. Each reflecting the eyes of the others. And of those others—you, too—behind the invisible wall, sitting and watching. The death-clock was ticking for you, *It's . . . time, it's . . . time,* and for you behind that you, *now . . . now, now . . . now.* Words were the least of it. Words of evasion: "Shall we take tea?" Of recognition: "Why? None of us likes tea." Ironic lies: "But in cases such as the one I have in mind, there are no witnesses." (Only the one witness?) And lying truths: "Nevertheless, the time sometimes comes when that which is most secret must be revealed, when the mask is stripped from the deceiver's face, when the identity of the criminal is exposed." (This deceiver?) Each looking at the others. Beata's condescending smile, the Baron's sidelong glance, Amelia's eyelids almost aching with effort (opening at last to the light?), the Colonel's impassive features registering a capitulation that meant defiance—and a sardonic confidence tightening the corners of your own mouth. Each of you evasively silent behind the mask of words. Each of you responsively silent behind the mask of evasive silence. "Silence hides nothing." (You kept on talking.) "Words conceal." (Talking, talking.) "We who sit here—we know who we are." (And rising in your throat an itch, an almost uncontrollable urge to croak like a parrot.) But watching the eyes behind the eyes—*now . . . now, now . . . now*—and almost glimpsing the actor-and-witness of your play.

> I think that I act; an "I" acts me,
> But all the time I am being dreamed by what-I-am.

So says Wei Wu Wei in *The Tenth Man.* But haven't you already evaded that recognition—with words? Otherwise the "I" who imagines himself director of this play, and self-directed actor in it, would have shriveled up and disappeared—or would have become just such a mask for . . . whom? . . .

as Hummel has been for you? Dürrenmatt must be right: *you can't go beyond the second scene of The Ghost Sonata.* For how can this noisy mind, with its itch to possess whatever plays through it, admit more than verbally the hidden meaning of our play?

Put out the light. Sleep.

FIVE

DREAMING
THE MUSIC

YOU SEEM wide awake tonight as you settle into your seats
and begin to scan the program, but you must be dreaming—
for what director in his right mind would dare to run these
three talky plays together in repertory? Yet there they are,
spelled out in black on green: *Three Sisters, Heartbreak House,*
and *Break of Noon*. And your ticket-stubs—M 12 and 13, just
left of center—are matched by two untorn pairs in your pocket.
   "Why?" you ask her. "What can be on his mind?"
   "Maybe the music," she says, without looking up. But what
music could link the wistful stammering of Chekhov's military
and provincial gentry, the paradoxical rhetoric of those Shavian
puppets who converge upon Shotover's landlocked ship, and
the lyric *tirades* of Claudel's impassioned souls somewhere in
the Far East? In your memory these scripts are separate worlds
—tacitly acknowledging each other's greatness, perhaps, across
thousands of miles of emptiness.
   Not that *Three Sisters* hasn't seemed disturbingly close to
your own life. A painfully amusing world, where affable and
weak-willed people are slowly overwhelmed by the triviality and
malignity of others. And why? Because a host of pressures and
distractions conspire to demand that resolute action be taken
just at the moment of extreme fatigue or even paralysis. You
recall how Irina, having fended off the ludicrously sinister
Solyony, must then face Natasha's demand that she give up her
own room. How Olga, worn out from helping the victims of
the fire, is unable to cope with Natasha's move to usurp all
household authority. How Chebutykin, after collapsing in self-
disgust, can only withdraw behind a mask of indifference as

Tusenbach goes to that fatal duel. "A comedy," Chekhov had declared—and with reason. Stanislavsky, of course, believed these people to be seeking "gaiety, laughter, animation" and freeing themselves inwardly from the banal. The far-off happiness of which Vershinin talks must therefore be present now—in aspiration or prophecy. And Soviet critics have since agreed. But how can they give so much weight to the mere words of these ineffective people? At most, you think, their closing speeches may sound a note of hope in a context that invites despair. As Chekhov said, art provides no answers: it states the problem—though this final dissonance, like the circular form of the entire play, seems to state a problem that defies solution. "Nothing matters," says Chebutykin. And Olga: "If only we knew, if only we knew." Not far, after all, from Chekhov to Beckett. Next year in Moscow? "Let's go," says one lonely voice to another. And they don't move.

Shaw's own world of heartbreak has seemed very different —despite his calling it a fantasia in the Russian manner. No impressionistic naturalism here, no iridescent and translucent surfaces, no disclosure of time's eroding of the will. Instead, a rhetorical farce—the accelerated education of Ellie in a Shavian wonderland where each puppet wears a mask or two grotesquely at odds with his own face. You recall Hector Hushabye, the romantic hero as kept man, reformer *manqué*, and part-time *raisonneur*, declaring: "In this house we know all the poses: our game is to find out the man under the pose." And Boss Mangan, self-made man and mama's boy, crying out like some ridiculous Lear: "Let's all strip stark naked." And Ellie Dunn, hardened by her final discovery that Shotover's seventh degree of concentration is only rum, agreeing with that more terribly absurd Lear that true happiness can come only when you are "stripped of everything, even of hope." Now, she says, "I want nothing." A much darker play than Shaw ever admitted—the probing of an emptiness about the heart. Some critics, of course, have seen purgation and renewal in that final explosion which destroys Mangan, the burglar, and the rectory. And Ellie, they say, survives heartbreak. But why then does she echo Hesione's wish for another bombing raid, another "glori-

ous experience?" Stripped of hope, this Cordelia lusts for
destruction. And what other end, you ask, does the play's own
erratic but self-cancelling dialectic permit? If the Prozorov
sisters in 1901 are already waiting for Godot, Shaw's chessmen
in 1916 are playing out an endgame. Shotover may say that
Hector's business as an Englishman is navigation—"learn it and
live; or leave it and be damned"—but this ship is foundering
in the void.

No doubt *Break of Noon* also moves toward a dark nothingness, but its self-stripping dialectic has seemed to you finally
less rhetorical than erotic. The tragic world of Racine transformed into a post-Wagnerian quartet? In which that bourgeois
Tristan, the priggish Mesa, must move from his shipboard encounter with Ysé at break of noon through his decision to commit adultery (and, in effect, murder) during the solar eclipse
and on to his acceptance of suffering and death at break of
midnight. *Partage de minuit* . . . which sheds a paradoxical
light of reunion. To break is to share? An absurdity here beyond Chekhov or Shaw: foolishness to the Greeks and the
moderns. But Christians, too, have doubted Claudel's extreme
theology of liberty and grace. *Etiam peccata*—even sin serves
—in the phrase from Augustine that Claudel used as epigraph
for *The Satin Slipper*. Shall I therefore sin boldly, and so construct my own cross—from which I can then address the God
whose priest I once thought to become? A doubtful cure for
the ego's religious pretensions. And the 1905 version of the
play, which suffuses Mesa's late speeches with pathos and
exaltation, seems especially self-deceptive on that score. But
that is the version most generally praised, even by those who
attack its ethics or theology, for it's easy to dismiss Claudel's
late and pathetic attempts to strip the lyricism from Act 3
when with Jean-Louis Barrault's collaboration he was preparing the play for production in 1948. Attempts that Barrault
himself sometimes found hard to take: after all, didn't he refuse
to give up the "*Cantique de Mesa*" that he'd already rehearsed?
And didn't he also cling to Mesa's last burst of eloquence—
"*moi-même / La forte flamme fulminante dans la gloire de
Dieu* . . ."? But the definitive text would cancel that speech, too.

Now, just before the time-bomb explodes, a wounded Mesa must painfully and silently reach for the light—encouraged by a flippant Ysé. Did Claudel's long dialogue between Animus and Anima have to come to that?

Which reminds you of her own rather flip reply: "Maybe the music." Did she mean Chekhov's counterpoint? Claudel's fascination with Wagner? Shaw's claim to have been a "pupil of Mozart"? Or something more obvious—like the receding strains of the military band at the end of *Three Sisters*, the "splendid drumming" in the sky near the end of *Heartbreak House* ("By thunder . . . ," exclaims Ellie, "it *is* Beethoven"), and that other Beethovenish muttering in the sky near the end of *Break of Noon* . . . the sound of the stars?

"Maybe what music?"

But she puts her finger to her lips: the lights are going down.

IMMEDIATELY the three of them: dark-blue, white, and black. Olga speaking. Olga in her teacher's uniform, moving about the drawing room with nervous lassitude, school-exercises in hand, wide awake but as if in a dream: "Father died just a year ago today. . . ." Speaking to whom? Expecting no answer from Irina, that shimmer of white lost in thought by the sunny window. Not even glancing toward Masha—your foreground figure, blackly ensconced in a downstage chair, hat on her lap, absorbed in a book. ". . . very cold and it was snowing. It seemed to me I would never live through it; and you were lying there quite still. . . ." Behind the upstage columns, just beyond your focus of attention, a maid beginning to lay the table in the ball-room. "And now—a year's gone by, and we talk about it so easily. . . ." We? Irina still not answering, Masha not looking up. Then the clock striking. You listen: how many of you listen? "The clock struck twelve then, too." Silence—in which you can almost hear . . . And now Olga recalling (for whom?) how the band played as they carried father to the cemetery.

"Why must we bring up all those memories?" Irina now speaking: part of a *we* that had been silently shared, after all,

but resisted? Masha still rather firmly not looking up. Refusing
to? Behind the columns, nearly inaudible to you, three men now
chatting. Olga turning to the window, exclaiming over the
spring warmth but at once going back to the past—to the spring
now eleven years ago when they left Moscow. This morning
her heart leapt with joy: she wanted so much to go home again.
"Go home to Moscow!" And a smile now playing over Irina's
face. From upstage, fragments of talk: "Small chance of that!"
"Of course, it's nonsense." Masha suddenly whistling a snatch
of yearning melody. A sharp reproof from Olga. Masha silent,
rigid. And now Olga recalling defensively her headaches, her
gloom, her weakness, day by day for the past four years.

   As you follow this increasingly intricate counterpoint of
echoes and reversals, abortive talk and shared silence, you
recall Gorky's verdict after a performance by the Moscow Art
Theater: "This is music—not acting." But it's a music, you now
begin to realize, that is itself a mode of action—and one that is
already unfolding its own meaning. Seldom confronting each
other directly, these people are always exchanging oblique responses, unacknowledged echoes, tacit resistances. Solitude is
certainly not—as some have called it—their essential condition.
Don't they allow a chronic inadvertence to distort or disrupt the
silent reciprocity of which they are all fitfully aware? (They?
But aren't they almost we—for you who sit silently with them?)
Even in turning away, they don't listen only to themselves. They
want to be aware of their distance from others, to hear themselves being absent from just this continuous music of existence
in which you find them immersed. Stanislavsky must have been
wrong: they don't want gaiety. They want to *want* gaiety. They
want to remain within some poignant dream of the past or of
the merely possible. But you were wrong, too: they aren't weak-
willed. Lost in thought, or addressing the air, or suddenly
whistling, they fix themselves in subtle opposition to the present. And yet, even the absence they seek has a consoling mutuality: "It seemed to me I would never live through it," Olga
had said; "and you had fainted and were lying there quite still,
just as if you were dead." Don't they want somehow to hear
themselves being absent together?

But in this resistance to a living present, what various life! There is Masha—remaining aloof even after the men come downstage, but radiating a blocked vitality that now speaks in those haunting lines from Pushkin: "A green oak grows by a curving shore, / And round that oak hangs a golden chain." And Chebutykin—now coyly giving Irina that most inappropriate samovar because he is still carrying on a fantasied romance with her dead mother. And Solyony—ostentatiously playing Lermontov or the sinister boor because of his painful shyness. (Just as the shy Natasha who is soon to enter will learn to play the domestic tyrant? What irrelevant moralism tempted you to think that pathetic pair more willful or malign than anyone else? Don't they simply escape into a different dream?) And there is the competent but glib Vershinin—now meeting the sisters, joking about the distant past or future, spinning out charming words so that he won't think of that histrionically suicidal wife who is a painful image of their shared condition, and increasingly glancing toward Masha. (And, yes, Masha has reversed her decision to leave the party. Won't the affair toward which they are already drifting—as she tries not to think of her histrionically pedantic husband—be their own dream of shared absence, a dream as hypnotic as those lines from Pushkin?) And now Andrey, the capable brother who has "such a bad habit"—as Olga has just told Vershinin—"always walking away." (For just that reason, Natasha's embarrassed running away from the luncheon table will soon easily trap him into proposing a domestic flight into shared absence.) And finally Kulygin—the leaden chain about Masha's green oak, maintaining himself precariously in the pompous academic dream toward which he had once tempted her schoolgirl romanticism. (And yet when he almost relaxes don't you glimpse through the mask an ironically compassionate eye?)

As the group moves into the ball-room for luncheon, leaving Irina behind with Tusenbach, you realize that you have neglected to place that ugly little lieutenant within this unfolding panorama of compulsive inadvertence. Is that because he seems the most genuinely attentive person in this drawing-room—

ready enough to join in with Vershinin's philosophizing, but ready also, as his remark to Irina now makes explicit, to understand even the Solyony who taunts him and will one day kill him? Surely Tusenbach doesn't want merely to *want* gaiety? But listen more closely as he now plays the perennially rejected lover: "Oh, I long so passionately for life, to work and aspire, and all this longing is part of my love for you, Irina." No, he hasn't even heard her say a moment ago that she doesn't want to hear such talk. Though aware of his own absurdity, he too wants to hear himself being absent—with her.

Now they have all gone behind the upstage columns, leaving the drawing-room appropriately empty. Fragments of talk reach you. Two lieutenants enter and take pictures of the various company. And is this, then, Chekhov's picture of our necessary condition? Can he do nothing but smilingly lament, with that Dr. Dorn in *The Sea Gull*: "But what can I do . . . ? Tell me, what can I do?" Many have said so—and you have agreed. Tolstoy, you recall, couldn't read many pages of *Three Sisters*. "Where does it all lead us?" he asked. But the script isn't the play, and the play is more than a picture. Hasn't it been inviting and requiring of you, through its increasingly panoramic focus and its developing counterpoint of disjunctive speeches and gestures, exactly what these people resist: that you open yourself to the full music of our existence in mutuality? In *Rosmersholm*, where you spy upon spying characters, the dramatic structure tempts you to join them in trying to possess the field of play as an intellectual object. But *Three Sisters* frustrates any such analytic observation—and even seems to empty you of that possessive "me." Detective work here would only distract from the revelatory pattern of present trivia. What happens instead? A widening of your peripheral attention, a listening in quiet alertness to the jagged texture of this music—and to the harmonies produced by the gestures through which these people construct for themselves a dream of shared need.

The play's style has been leading you into an alternative mode of witnessing—a norm rendered more subtly and immediately than if it were consigned to a *raisonneur* like Krouschov in *The Wood Demon*. And witnessing, as you have seen, is itself a fundamental action. Josiah Royce said somewhere, "Finite beings are always such as they are in virtue of an *inattention* which at present blinds them to their actual relations to God and to one another." Leaving "God" aside, as it seems, *Three Sisters* explores something like that intuition. In their willed inattention, its people experience one another as distant or nonexistent. They experience space as constriction or separation, time as a not-yet or a slipping-away, the world itself as the constant threat of nothingness. But through you the play has been disclosing time and space as an expanding *now*, a moving yet simultaneous apprehension of these variously self-closed subjective worlds which are really one.

And yet, have you really been an empty alertness to the "now?" Haven't you limited your attention to a poignantly realistic fiction, to what you call the "people" in that drawing-room? But those "people" are living masks for the actors, whose attention to your present field has alerted you to the more abortive reciprocity that they are playing—and so enabling you indirectly to play. At this moment Andrey and Natasha seem lost in their awkward embrace, unaware of the newly arrived officers who stare in amusement. But the actors are sharing with you that quietly farcical closing tableau, in which years of pain are ironically implicit. Stanislavsky knew very well the great importance of "public solitude" as a technique for the Chekhovian actor. And he also knew that the actor must sustain, while "penetrating into the most secret places" of his character's heart, an "unbroken flow" of communion with his stage partners, with objects, and with the audience. Only a style founded upon such communion can enable the cast of *Three Sisters* to present, within and beyond these masks of distraction and self-obsession, our mutual immanence.

Of course, for the actors and for you, the play's apparent realism combines its intimate penetration with a clarifying distance. Could you hear this music if immersed in it as Tusenbach must be? But then isn't your own point of view itself an absurd fiction, the contemplative equivalent of what the characters more damagingly seek? If so, you must now be experiencing your own version of the play's "spine" or objective: to hear ourselves being absent from the silent music of presence. You stop short. Does *Three Sisters* ask you to abandon the theater— in order to become genuinely present to your own life? "I saw a wonderful play last night," says Lopakhin in *The Cherry Orchard.* "It was so funny." To which Lyubov retorts: "It probably wasn't funny at all. Instead of going to plays, you should take a good look at yourself. . . ." Advice, certainly, which that histrionic lady might better take than give!

But despite such ambivalences in Chekhov's homeopathic art, which seeks to cure illusion through illusion, your own life is nowhere but *here* for the moment. And this performance is now inviting you to open yourself more fully. In the second act, Andrey will tell Natasha that there's nothing to talk about and will then confess his disappointment to the deaf Ferapont. Masha and Vershinin will exchange flattering complaints about tedious men and complaining wives. Tusenbach, who dreams of work, will chatter of his patience to an Irina who thinks only of the exhaustion to which her own dream of work has led. Vershinin will pretend to debate Tusenbach about the existence of happiness, and Chebutykin will squabble with Solyony about whether a roast is a roast or an onion is an onion. And, after Tusenbach has got drunk to prepare for a night of trashy piano-playing that Natasha has already vetoed, after Solyony has forced words of love and Natasha words of maternal anxiety upon the perturbed Irina, Olga will bring to the tired and frustrated company a splitting headache and the report that the whole town is talking of Andrey. But you? You will have to listen closely to the counterpoint between all this inattentive loquacity and the action of performance itself.

Through an evasive complaining or yearning that nourishes the very predicaments on which it feeds, the characters will increasingly justify their sense of being helpless victims of cir-cumstance. But the actors, by rendering the nuances of this subtext with such affectionate realism, will utterly transform each instance of self-closure—from Natasha's and Andrey's non-conversation to the final moments in which Irina ignores Kulygin, who ignores Vershinin, who ignores Olga, who ignores everyone. As the characters confirm their prisons, sometimes thinking of an illusory key called "tomorrow," the actors will be leading you to understand from the inside—in all their tempting ease or seeming necessity—those momentary maneuvers of turning off or away that enable us gradually to construct some trap of habit, addiction, or catastrophic role-playing from which no ordinary act of attention can then free us. And won't your own painful exhilaration, as the second act sputters to its close, indicate that you will have doubly shared the spectrum of self-isolating moods generated here by such maneuvers: the self-pity of Andrey and Chebutykin, the fatuous if self-ironic verbosity of Vershinin, Tusenbach, and Kulygin, the cruel petulance of Natasha and Solyony, the hysterical indecisiveness of Masha, the sick anxiety of Olga, and the numb exhaustion of Irina?

You will then be prepared to act and witness, in the context appropriately provided by a disastrous fire of unknown origin, some yet more painful consequences of that willed and often quite lucid inattention. Most obviously, of course, in the generous but weary Olga—who will withdraw from Natasha's rude attack into a near faint, leave the room to avoid the spectacle of the drunken Chebutykin, block out Masha's literary confession of love by insisting from behind a night-screen that she can't hear, and finally utter no word at all from behind that screen as Andrey makes his defiant confession of guilt. But the despairing Irina, too, will now be merely curt with Chebutykin, won't notice for some time that Tusenbach has fallen asleep, and will say nothing in response to either Masha's confession or Andrey's. And even Masha, who so eagerly answers Vershinin's snatch of song, will then dismiss Tusenbach and Kulygin in bored irritation, sit in silence as Olga consoles Irina, confess her love in phrases intended mainly for her own ears, and walk out (again answering Vershinin's music) just as Andrey proposes a family conference. Won't Irina's pleading curtain-line sum up for you then, not just her desire to escape from their shared predicament, but also the interior action that has repeatedly constituted that predicament? "Let's go!"

The last act, of course, will bring that performed action full circle—to an unresolved dissonance. The military band will play, Chebutykin will hum, and the sisters will utter their various cries, as ex-lieutenant Tusenbach is now carried to the cemetery. But the action of performance, far from being circular, will have moved through an expanding present to disclose all that was implicit in the play's opening scene. And suddenly you foresee, just before the end, a moment of harmony between the music so imperfectly known by the *dramatis personae* and that being disclosed through the play's total form of acting and witnessing. Thanks to Solyony's catastrophic role-playing, thanks also to the repeatedly endorsed decorum of evasion that lets affairs of "honor" as well as "love" proceed as if unnoticed, death is now imminent. And amid a conversation designed mainly to hide from each other and from themselves their full awareness of such a possibility, Tusenbach will turn to Irina —and he who plays Tusenbach will turn to her who plays Irina—and say: "Really, I feel fine. I feel as if I were seeing those pine trees and maples and birches for the first time in my life. They all seem to be looking at me, waiting for something." And they are. They are waiting for Tusenbach to wake up from your daily sleepwalking. They are inviting you to listen. . . .

And you turn to her: "The music of silence?"

◆◆◆◆◆◆◆◆◆◆◆◆◆◆◆◆

A SKILLFUL feint with that teetering tray of empty bottles— a near crash?—and then in a brisk stage-Irish: "God bless us! Sorry to wake you, miss, I'm sure . . . but you are a stranger to me. What might you be waiting here for now?"

And the pert ingénue, a disarming life roused beneath her polite indignation: "Waiting for somebody to show *some* signs of knowing that I have been invited here."

Who answers whom? Though Ellie Dunn seems to have waked with a start as Nurse Guinness was breezing past with those rum-bottles, she may still be dreaming. The playing style, a cheerful burlesque of drawing-room comedy, offers no clue— but at least it's inviting *you* into the game. And the set—a crazy part-house, part-ship, beams jutting askew, against a backdrop that might be sky or earth or void—tells you that Shaw's fairly realistic specifications have been jettisoned in favor of a design

more appropriate to the script. This is leaky architecture that
has become aggressive rhetoric that has become its own symbol.
This "silly house," Ellie will call it, "this strangely happy house,
this agonizing house, this house without foundations." Already
you know that it isn't just a Sussex country house, or the nineteenth-century British tradition on the rocks, or the whole of
Europe on the edge of doom. It is Shaw's house—and yours.
Where does this possible dream take place? In the theater. And
it will be no leisurely prelude but a self-questioning scherzo.

From every part of the stage, the Shavian ventriloquism begins to shape your world. But as you enter that sequence of
duels or duets you recall from the script—Hesione Hushabye's
sweetly condescending chat with Ellie about a British Othello
who is really Hector on the make, Captain Shotover's brusque
attempts to persuade Boss Mangan that he's much too old for
Ellie, Hector's knowingly empty flirtation with that dangerously
conventional woman who likes to be called Lady Utterword, and
then his shrewdly mad conversation with Shotover about human vermin, vampire women, and every decent man's need to
kill, kill, kill, kill, kill—the action now seems radically changed
by the sheer fact of performance. These rhetorical puppets,
though certainly not Chekhovian "people" whose depths you
might penetrate, have nonetheless a surprisingly rich vitality.
How had Shaw put it? *The puppet is the actor in his primitive
form. Its symbolic costume . . . , its unchanging stare . . . , the
mimicry by which it suggests human gesture in unearthly
caricature—these give to its performance an intensity to which
few actors can pretend.* But on this all too human stage, of
course, each actor is in fact playing several puppets—for the
characters of *Heartbreak House* are schizoid embodiments of
theatricality itself: stock-company "lines" who are also operatic parts, dream figures, semi-allegorical personages, and oc-
casional voices of what may pass for Shavian wisdom. . . . *my
plays require a special technique of acting, . . . in particular
great virtuosity in sudden transitions of mood that seem to the
ordinary actor to be transitions from one "line" of character
to another.* On such a stage a heartbroken adolescent can in-
stantly become a cynic on the prowl, a maternal confidante can

also be a seductive hostess and an emasculating wife, a philandering lapdog can be a shrewd judge of character and an off-stage hero, and a mad hatter can be a mad Lear and a mad Shaw.

Nor are these merely the masks of a clowning playwright. Each actor is grounding a brittle and ironic multiplicity of roles in his or her own protean life—and in yours. Isn't that the initial meaning of this play's cheerfully heartbreaking invitation? Through the knowing poses of Hushabye bohemianism, the deadpan bombast of Shotover's apocalyptic or merely defensive joking, and the grotesquely abrupt stages of Ellie's breakdown and self-transcendence, the actors are inviting you to join them in the kaleidoscopic theater of your shared conditioning. Each puppet-role cries out in the voice of its temporary host: "Look! Play *me* now! Haven't you done so long enough without admitting it?" But as one piece after another is added to the game, as you delightedly expose your own Hectoring romanticism, your capitalist Bossism, your Mazzini idealism—where are you going? "Is it quite understood," says Lady Utterword with a superb smile, "that we are only playing?" "Quite," responds Hector on the instant. "I am deliberately playing the fool, out of sheer worthlessness." Do puppets, characters, and actors there speak for you all? . . . *the play began with an atmosphere and does not contain one word that was foreseen before it was written.* . . . You can almost believe it—despite the ghost of a double plot that will take Ellie on the rebound from Hector to Mangan to Shotover while Ariadne, shadowed by her brother-in-law, toys with Hector. And certainly this buoyant improvisation is not, like *Three Sisters*, unfolding some silent richness of meaning already implicit in its opening moments. Isn't its agitation disturbingly static? Isn't the play itself a landlocked yet foundering dreamship?

But wait: . . . *it is not in the nature of things possible for a person to take in a play fully until he is in complete possession of its themes.* . . . And that Shavian principle applies even to this unpremeditated music. Don't you already hear in the romantic, political, and moral directionlessness of your playing an anxious search for direction? A desire to find the necessary limits of your own lively negation? As each character helps to strip the others in the game that Hector will define, won't actors and witnesses be implicitly trying to exhaust what challenges and entertains? What puppet-role *can't* be exposed or exploded? What ship or house might constitute a *true* image of the private and public thing—a truly moral economy? Surely the performed action, in its indirect search for direction, will be almost at one with the action of performance. These *dramatis personae* constitute a many-layered mask for a playful heart— a protean life not Shaw's alone—that has committed itself to words, to ideas, to power, and has become profoundly uneasy. Pressing back on yourself now in negation after negation, exposing the ironic impotence of each bold critique, delighting in the emptiness of each attack upon your own false solidities, you must follow an unpredictable path. In *Three Sisters* the pattern of resonating coincidences had a formal inevitability, but here the most necessary consequences must be strange leaps. Nothing is certain but the gradually deepening darkness —in which you *play* the leaps.

Doesn't this become boldly explicit at the end of Act 1, when the conversation suddenly transforms itself? Shotover raises a strange wail in the darkness: "What a house! What a daughter!" Hesione raves: "What a father!" And Hector echoes in mockery: "What a husband!" Then Shotover bellows: "Is there no thunder in heaven?" And Hector—playing with that lofty Shakespearean mode: "Is there no beauty, no bravery on earth?" And Hesione: "What do men want? . . ." Their grotesque litany or mock-tragic chorus then modulates into a weird chant which Shotover begins—"I builded a house for my daughters, and opened the doors thereof, / That men might come for their choosing, and their betters spring from their love"—and which Hector and Hesione pick up and complete in a neatly rhymed stanza. The abrupt shift into half-parodied lyricism has betrayed and partly expressed an uneasiness about your previous path through self-negating but self-delighting rhetoric. Isn't the darkness really deeper than that? Another shift into the flat sardonic—Ariadne calls and Shotover comments: "The cat is on the tiles"—and you suddenly feel in this play an eerie depth that no character or player seems likely to plumb. Hector goes into the hall: "Shall I turn up the lights for you?" And Shotover declaims madly—for all of you: "No. Give me deeper darkness. Money is not made in the light." The comic inadequacy of that aphorism increases your feeling that what's now in question is a darkness that may be quite literally unspeakable.

An end to words—amid this linguistic exuberance? But what else? Early in the second act the speechifying Boss Mangan, who has exposed his rascality in an effort to make Ellie break off their engagement, finds himself reduced by her hypnotic powers to a mutely listening fat body. After overhearing talk that greatly disturbs his precious "I," he is roused from that semi-trance only to be reduced to childish tears by Hesione. Then, during a farcical interlude, a fake burglar so plays upon the inauthentic liberalism of the propertied classes that he reduces everyone to an awkward if momentary silence. And soon even Shotover's pretensions to Shavian wisdom are punctured by Ellie: "Now I have found you out," she says. "You pretend to be busy, and think of fine things to say, and run in and out to surprise people by saying them, and get away before they can answer you." Whereupon she proceeds more gently to hypnotize him toward a spiritual marriage. By the end of this act, the once imperturbable Randall Utterword has himself been reduced by Ariadne's verbal whirlwind to foaming madness and tears. At least female words are now overcoming male words—as if in some bitter expansion of that final moment in *Man and Superman* when Ann Whitefield tells the revolutionist Tanner whom she has ensnared, "Keep on talking, dear"—to the accompaniment of "universal laughter."

But the next leap? Mustn't this play answer Ellie, too? ". . . I feel now as if there was nothing I could not do," she has said to Shotover, "because I want nothing." But as she then proclaimed the self-sufficiency of one stripped of everything, even of hope, you saw her almost unconsciously grip the old man's hand in hers. Finally, of course, it is not a question of sexual superiority. You know that in the third act, having exploded all male pretensions, the Eternal Woman will herself call for more bombs. Haven't we found ourselves out? Through whatever mask, we enact the same predicament. Appalled by the futility of our commitment to words, ideas, and power, we remain hypnotized by our own verbal agitation. Puppets of ourselves, we keep on talking. Trying to talk each other into silence. To talk *ourselves* into silence.

A moonless night. It is Act 3. Your comic masks, rather the worse for wear, appear in the garden. Somewhere in the darkness a voice that once was Boss Mangan's begins to whimper. "Silence!" orders Captain Shotover, *fortissimo*. "I say, let the heart break in silence!" Yes. And that moment, so refreshing in its evident absurdity, can't be negated, you think, by anything to come. Not by the "splendid drumming" in the sky, or the explosion of the dynamite that Shotover has saved to "blow up the human race if it goes too far," or the brightness blazing from the windows of the house as Hector, like some spirit of Enlightenment gone berserk, races through the rooms tearing down curtains and lighting lamps. The noisy brilliance of our self-cancelling rhetoric now points only to what it tries to hide—the dark silence of heartbreak.

You can understand why Bernard Dukore has called this play a panorama of "existential damnation." And why Charles Berst has said that its "Tolstoyan, Christian, Shavian judgment" is colored by "the playwright's profound agony at his own insignificance and powerlessness." You can even understand why Maurice Valency has read it as a "masochist" fantasy that derives "its romantic charm and all its cogency as drama" from "the death wish." But such judgments surely result from the hasty abstraction of dark notes in the performed action that could never in themselves account for the full music of your shared action of performance. Was Francis Fergusson closer to the mark? Is this a play of "sharply rationalizing" and "fully awake" characters, set forth by a playwright who has virtually become an "inspired clown" with a "disinterested vision of action as a rationalizing in the void"? No: these Shavian puppets remain locked in their Hushabye dreamhouse, and the action of performance is no external relation between a clowning Shaw and yourselves. Actors and witnesses, only a bit more wakeful than the puppets they play, are here becoming alert to their shared dreams. This present action, no rationalizing in the void, is an undoing of your masks of competence and sophistication—an undoing shaped by a playful awareness of what such refreshingly "self"-destructive laughter allows you to celebrate.

A teetering play of empty puppets—a near crash—and an unpremeditated feat of balance. As if in playing the nothingness of your words of power—and chiefly, perhaps, of the "I" that calls up the entire dream of heartbreak—you are awakened to . . . some sign of being invited? Why else could Shaw, years later, let King Charles answer George Fox's attack on "mummery, whether in playhouse or steeplehouse," with that dry question: "Have you considered, Pastor, that the playhouse is a place where two or three are gathered together?"

"Shaw was right," you whisper before the lights come up, "to call this his greatest play. It answers all his words."

~~~~~~~~~~~~

IT IS already late in Act 3. It is dark. After prelude and scherzo, now a swift finale? In this half-destroyed Confucian temple where a time-bomb will soon end everything—no, in what *was* that temple before its battered walls dissolved a few moments ago, opening the action to the starry night—a man, propped in a large and shabby armchair, faces you. Almost, as if glimpsed in some distorting and revealing mirror, the actor's double and yours? For you have been sharing his conversation with the silence, and with the low muttering of the stars that sometimes articulates the silence. Suddenly he senses behind him—don't you hear the breath being held?—that other to whom he had refused to give himself and who had then abandoned him. Is he awake? Dreaming? Her lineaments gradually disengage themselves from the darkness. And then she speaks.

During this conversation, this hesitant reunion of Mesa and Ysé, the entire play seems to draw together, not merely on stage but among you and within you. For the action here is dissolving your common-sense distinctions between "outer" and "inner" space. More definitely than *Three Sisters, Break of Noon* has been unfolding the meaning of a silence implicit in its opening moments. And more firmly than *Heartbreak House*, this play has been seeking the limits of its own inadequate verbalism. It's as if your shared playing has moved, through an intersubjectivity that is now painfully beginning to understand its incarnate condition, its confinement within reciprocally dependent centers of perception, toward an end that calls through the silence. Is that why the performed action and the action of performance here compose neither a counterpoint of opposites, as in *Three Sisters*, nor a vexed identity, as in *Heartbreak House*, but a gradual convergence?

The performed action itself has obviously converged toward the Omega, the love-trap and death-trap, that you have seen with increasing clarity in the ship of Act 1, the Chinese tomb of Act 2, and this armchair of Act 3 where Ysé is now sitting with a Mesa who finds it strangely unnecessary to look at her. ("The end of the world," he had once said half-believingly, "is always imminent.") At break of noon the ship held four homeless and light-struck passengers, each fleeing the disillusionments of the past, each seeking a satisfaction that meant the risk of death. "All of us dead and buried next year, my little friends," said Amalric then, as they passed Suez. "There is no place where we could stop if we wanted to," said Mesa. And yet, impelled by a restless passion within their various kinds of adventuring, what could they really want but that impossible *end*? Amalric with a masculine bravado that needs repeatedly to prove itself, de Ciz with a feminine deviousness that hides his commercial appetite, Mesa with a self-righteous diffidence that defends his ego, and Ysé with all the contradictoriness of a Philistine *femme fatale* who desires both mastery and subjection, solid goods and an unattainable ecstasy—each of the four was ready in self-blinded pursuit to exploit and abandon the others. But because Mesa and Ysé could hear, through what seemed most opposite, withheld, forbidden, the silent call of their identity, they would meet again between the claws of the Chinese tomb, during the eclipse. Stripping themselves of name and responsibility, sending de Ciz to his death (though with his wry acquiescence), they knew the perversity of their death-longing, but not that it might become a moment in the self-transcending dialectic of their passion. Now, after mutual betrayal and consequent suffering, aware of the nothingness that insists on possessing the world, they are discovering through each other their true names. They sometimes speak, of course, with a childish petulance and pride that you find rather embarrassing, for this performance is following the "definitive" text of 1949. But isn't this frank recognition of the still clinging self preferable, after all, to the magniloquence Claudel had once allowed his alter-ego—which he must have cancelled as he listened more closely to the end that now seems to have evoked this entire play as response?

Claudel's severe pruning of his own elevated rhetoric was surely consonant—whatever his literary admirers may say—with the larger collaborative process that transformed his mono-logical closet drama of 1905 into a genuine theatrical event. Thanks to the gradually self-transcending playing-style that Claudel worked out with Barrault, the action of performance has been converging with the performed action toward the same silent end. Like the *dramatis personae*, the actors and witnesses seem also to have been stripping away the accidents of time and space and the resistances of self-will as they discover their essential mutuality. In Act 1, when the four characters con-fronted one another in enigmatically distanced intimacy—look-ing at each other's faces, said Amalric, "as if we were playing poker and the cards are dealt"—you too were distanced from them and from each other by the appearances of an "external" space and time. Beginning and ending with a frozen tableau like an old photograph, Act 1 was a framed image of the past in memory, which moved from its opening at four bells through a center of mutual recognition at six bells ("What is there be-tween you and me?" "Mesa, I am Ysé") to its conclusion at eight bells or noon. And just as two of those four characters hesitantly began to communicate *through* the external appear-ances—most notably in that long exchange through the eyes that reduced Mesa to an embarrassed and angry stammering before Ysé—so the playing style allowed the lyric *tirades* to filter only hesitantly through a "bourgeois realism" of every-

day gestures, establishing a fragmentary musical communication from actors to witnesses of nuances that ordinary talk must
leave to the gaps between words. In effect, didn't you then
share Mesa's position, as Amalric described it? "Rather than
looking directly at you, he seems to be looking at you somewhere else in a mirror. He listens to you from somewhere else
—from where your voice resounds." It was strange how the
"realism" that usually claims to signify immediacy could there
provide the distance, the set of baffles, separating you from one
another—as if you were essentially more than any "realistic"
surfaces could disclose, beings to whom only a poetic reality
could adequately respond. You began to understand why
Claudel—as Barrault had said—was interested during revision
and production "not only in his text but in the smallest gestures, concerning which he is full of ideas." His highly verbal
and egocentric text was moving, through this encounter with
the medium of theatrical reciprocity, toward an actualizing of
its own full meaning.

As Act 2 began to move beyond that "realism," it took the
performed action a step closer to your field of play. Opening
with Mesa's long soliloquy while waiting for Ysé in the center
of the tomb, it seemed no image of the past but a present reality: more immediate yet more boldly stylized. Gestures and
utterances now began to compose a coherent music. All bodily
expression tended to become, at least during the solar eclipse,
a vehicle for a silent invisibility. You recall the long moment
of Mesa's approach to Ysé from behind, his hands going deli-
cately all over her body without touching her. "Someone is
behind me whom I can't see," said Ysé, "and who has come to
me from I don't know where." And that other moment at mid-
eclipse—"There is no tomorrow," said Mesa—when with
clasped hands the two almost danced their twistingly mutual
approach. At such moments the reciprocal play of actor and
actress for the witnesses was no less evident than the reciprocity
between Mesa and Ysé. But as if such immediacy were possible only in darkness, the act then moved back toward a more
distancing "realism" in the oblique conversation with de Ciz—

and so to its ironic curtain gesture: the backslapping embrace of betrayal offered by Mesa.

Though Act 3 began with a rather similar evening conversation between Ysé and Amalric in their doomed domesticity amid the ruins of the besieged temple, it has swiftly moved beyond all but the barest indications of "realism" toward this darkness illuminated by points of light, this living space in which you now participate: neither "external" nor "internal" but a shared vision almost out of time. (For now it has become true: there is no tomorrow.) That swift transformation of style was assisted, during Amalric's temporary absence from the stage, by Mesa's first long address to the seemingly unresponsive Ysé. Speaking again from behind her, he recapitulated and re-enacted his year of suffering in her absence. ("She is close by, and yet she isn't. She is here but she is not here. . . . Like someone who knows and says with her lips, 'be silent!' ") For you as for Mesa, time and space there became aspects of a present dialogue with silence. And after the fight with Amalric —during which Ysé already began to move in spirit back toward the Mesa whom she was abandoning—and after Amalric and Ysé had propped him in this chair, the ruined walls could quite easily dissolve to enable you to share a dialogue with a vaster and yet more responsive silence. (For while pruning the rhetoric of Act 3, Claudel also introduced the articulate sound of the stars. Why? In Beethoven, as he insisted to Barrault, there is always the music that speaks and the music that listens. And so in each of us, for our experience is essentially dialogical. More clearly heard, the operatic "*Cantique de Mesa*" had therefore to be transformed from a monologue, in which a potentially self-deceptive communication with "silence" might seem to Mesa sufficient, into an authentic dialogue with that Other who transcends any empirical consciousness. Hence the "stellar kettle" has muttered, for you also, "The others . . . the others . . . .") Nevertheless, those theatrical transitions would have been impossible gimmicks if they had not been in harmony with the self-transforming style of playing. Speech in this Act has been yet more clearly silence-filled, and more resonant. The recurrent patterns of gesture that so interested Claudel—the exchange of gazes, the address to the silent partner, the attitude of expectancy, the silent lip-speech, the joined and slowly raised hands—are now unfolding their full meaning. It's as if you and the *dramatis personae* could now participate openly in a previously hidden music. You recall Claudel's interest in the Nō, where each rhythmic gesture discloses a meaning. For actors and witnesses, Claudel said in his *Journal*, "Nō is a school of patience, of tension, and of attention." And suddenly that sentence from *Ecclesiasticus* comes to mind—his real motto: *Ne impedias musicam*. Don't hinder the music.

Let it play through you—toward what end? Toward a dramatic actualizing of our mutual immanence, of what Charles Williams called our co-inherence, as we approach that strangely absent Presence . . . "someone who in myself may be more truly myself than I." At this moment in a play that has increasingly seemed an implicit celebration of Tenebrae, you don't need to recall Mesa's agonized talk in Act 1 about a Witness who "never leaves me for a minute's peace," or Ysé's less self-involved remark in Act 3: "Yes, Amalric, when we walk, our foot makes a sound. It's as if you are walking in the night and you can't see clearly. But there is a wall on the right somewhere." Hasn't the play itself, through its shared and convergent patterns of gesture, gone very far indeed toward rendering the strictly un-dramatizable presence of a silent Host in your midst, with whom you are essentially in dialogue? As Mesa has recognized the silence that speaks through the other who holds the clue to his being, so Ysé has recognized in her return to Mesa the life-in-death that she has always sought. And so, opening your-selves to your assigned roles as actors and witnesses, listening to what speaks in this situation, you too have been led by a seemingly unpremeditated but increasingly graceful playing to understand the ominous line now spoken through Ysé: "You could die by my hand."

Slowly she stands up behind Mesa, raising her arm by easing successively each joint and finally the hand. And she asks for the stars. "I can't unhook them for you," says Mesa. And she:

"It's easy. Just stretch out your hand." He is still a miser. Are they forbidden? Take them. Give them to me. . . . Childish requests? A still possessive Ysé? No: the play's recognition that light-struck beings in time can experience no moment of satisfied arrival but only a continued participation in the necessary breaking . . . .

"It's easy. Just stretch out your hand. Get up.' Taking his hand, she forces him painfully to stand erect, to lift his hand yet higher. Against the darkness they shape with their raised and joined hands the sign of the end that has drawn them here. "Be quiet," he says. But she answers, sinking down at his feet, "Remember me for one moment in this darkness. I was once your vine." Now you can see only a luminous raised hand. And now the curtain drops like lightning.

It is still quite dark—but that's no stellar kettle muttering in the distance. The five-o'clock train, it must be, clanking across the bridge over the river. Reminding you somehow of that journey of discovery taken by protagonist and reader in Butor's *Modification*. And must you now awake from this dream of performance to write a fiction about three talky plays, three pieces of music, three ways of listening to the silence? Though you can't see her face, there in the darkness, wouldn't she smile at the thought? You—to play?

SIX

UNDOING

Dramatis Personae
PLAYER KING
PLAYER QUEEN
SACRIFICED PAWN
WITNESS
and those who happen to play them

An apparently empty stage, in darkness. At the rear, a large two-panelled mirror forms a dimly visible wall. Spot comes up on the PLAYER KING, *downstage left. Eleventh-century robe and coronet; no scabbard. He stands looking off into the wings as he wipes a sword absently across his sleeve. Then he turns —hectic red on the pale cheeks, a forelock of too vividly yellow hair—and fixes his eyes on us.*

PLAYER KING:

Yes—"here we are . . . together . . . forever." Words intended less for those young fools who played my counsellors tonight than for you, my fellow-prisoners. This throne-room, this narrow stage, this cell— But why, at this late moment in our history, do I need to imitate that Richard II who so laboriously studied how he might compare the prison where he lived unto the world? Richard's cell, as Ionesco has now remarked, is the cell of all our solitudes. This *is* the world, and we are here.

Shall we spell out the trap? Or has it been made quite clear enough by this play of lucid madness which I might almost have written? Perhaps did write, for I recall dreams in which I was no Germanic emperor but Pirandello himself. A grotesque tragedy—no?—of a nameless man condemned to play forever, and in full awareness of his absurdity, the petty ambitions and jealousies of this fake Henry IV. Condemned, but not as you may think. That sword-thrust into Belcredi a moment ago, like Hamlet's through an arras once, was hardly decisive. A symptom, yes—and a strong curtain. But what action other than *this* (*indicating his own aspect*) was ever possible for one who has awakened from years of unconscious fixation only to discover that life has passed him by, and that the very rival who had ridden behind him during some fatuous masquerade twenty years ago has now become for *her*—no, for what she now *thinks* herself to be—a foul parody of what he himself—agh!

But that's not it. ". . . do you suppose I am going to trouble myself any more," as I said to them, "about what happened between us . . . the share you had in my misfortune with her . . . the part he now has in your life?" No: *had* in her life, for Belcredi is now well out of it. The Marchioness Matilda herself might now almost be . . . my widowed mother. And how could such as I have ever assumed any serious role in a world that is trapped in the madness to which I have awakened? He who knows that every "I" is a false identity, an unconscious fixation on an image of the past, must choose to remain the quietly lucid caricature of our predicament—if only in revenge against life's beautiful beliefs. Belcredi, indeed! And life itself, in any event, will force him to do so—will set loose upon him a pack of stupid puppets who for their own gratification will try to cure him and will drive him into such a rage that—! (*Catching himself, he throws down the sword in disgust; then faces us again with a blandly pedagogical smile.*)

Enough. The play has amply elucidated my situation—having cast me, after all, as my own *raisonneur*. But you may have defended yourselves as usual against its claim that my situation is also yours. Didn't you, in fact, dismiss some parts of its demonstration as mere lapses in dramatic craft? No doubt the gentlemen who occupied those now vacant seats on the aisle are already at their typewriters complaining once again that Doctor Genoni is too easy a burlesque of psychiatry, that the Marchioness is a fascinating woman whose dramatic possibilities are forgotten by Pirandello halfway through the play, that her daughter Frida and young di Nolli are embarrassingly empty,

and that Tito Belcredi seems more substantial only because my
colleague's self-ironic drawl manages to speak volumes without
committing itself to anything. But their reviews tomorrow will
be effective admissions that their own firm sense of identity
prevents them from understanding a realistic play that contains
no *characters* at all. None. *Henry IV* gives the stage to thirteen
unknown actors who are in search of that solidity which the
term "character" suggests. When did we ever stop our hackneyed
improvising? And when will we learn to say with my masked
relative in *It Is So (If You Think So)*, "for myself, I am nothing"?

We have tried—each in his own way—to cope with the madness of unconscious role-playing by deliberately playing our
roles. And what may have seemed a confused exposition was a
swift sketch of our various strategies. When those two valets
jumped into position as if caught unprepared by the opening
curtain, they announced the most basic level of our play: as
actors in this theater tonight we would confront *your* unconscious role-playing with an apparent realism. And the fake
throne-room of Goslar, with its modern and life-sized portraits
flanking the antique throne, declared our method: a dialectical
clash of seeming realities.

At once we outlined the moves in our theatrical game, which
is also yours, by playing it lightly. For the young men who
played counsellors in order to cope with my presumed madness were the obviously masked servants of our compulsively
timeless *commedia dell'arte*. Because a Tito has died—as one
would die at the end of our play—Berthold must be initiated.
Two basic moves, there: "learning the new role" and "hazing
the new player." Why the hazing? Don't pretend ignorance.
Why did I feel that irresistible urge, a few moments ago, to lift
the screaming Frida in my arms? Why do I hear myself even
now adopting this condescending tone? Insecure within a scenario that requires us to improvise our identity, we fall back on
our apparent identity as actors—and solidify *that* role by pro-
ducing a play-within-the-play intended to transform our more
vulnerable colleagues into comic marionettes. That's why those
uneasy counsellors began to tease old John when that naive
player, so enviably identified with his primary role as servant,

entered in modern evening clothes. And their brief conflict
sketched two further moves in the game: "invading the play as
an agent of the real" and "defencing the play by incorporating
the invader." With those moves and *la parole facile*, couldn't
one write plays like *Hay Fever* and *Who's Afraid of Virginia
Woolf?* till the end of the century? A thought that makes one
thirst for our final—and yet useless—move, which was soon
demonstrated by Berthold: "trying to escape from this play of
madness." But by then, more serious players had entered to
perform their combinations and permutations of those moves.

The most serious among us try to hide their own theatricality
—even from themselves. Hypnotized by his own pompous
phrases, Doctor Genoni becomes the stock pedant of our *commedia*, who wants to end the playing of others by imposing his
own solemn script. And young di Nolli shares that kind of illusion: he's nothing but the attempt to play the stuffily regal
notion of his own seriousness—filial piety, marital responsibility. But his fiancée is more intriguing—terrified of this madness of playing, exactly because she knows its secret fascination. Remember her haste to put on that old costume of the
Marchioness which now threatens to prevent her from breath-
ing? Wouldn't she love to *be* now what her mother claims to
have been? Ha! in their earnest desire to *be*, those two *ingénus*
succeed in becoming nothing more than replicas of those portraits on the wall.

But if we recognize the theatricality of all seriousness—without, of course, taking ourselves any less seriously—the masks
become more complex. The Marchioness and Belcredi prefer
the ironic roles of aging *femme fatale* and sophisticated fool.
They want to be known as playing the game lightly—and, within
that script, to claim an ambiguous "sincerity." Your own
more shrewdly whimsical Genoni, Doctor Berne, might diagnose
them as players of "Greenhouse" and "Perversion." The
Marchioness scorned my own glaring insistence, years ago,
exactly because it threatened the defensive triviality that Belcredi respected through his mockingly hostile maneuvers. And
yet, behind her brilliant mask, what is she but a hysterical
image of lost youth? How swiftly she drew attention to her por-

trait by finding Frida there instead of herself—and so managed
to possess retrospectively both portrait and daughter! And after
these players had decided (with a touchingly naive histrionic
delight!) to invade and explode my own play—only to be cast
by me, of course, in yet another play designed to catch their
consciences—did you notice how vulnerable the Marchioness
became to my obliquely nostalgic probing? In Act 3, after their
crude attempt at psychodrama, her complicated game almost
vanished—to the disappointment of the reviewers who adore
such tricks—and she became little more than a poignant wish
for simplicity. Wouldn't she soon have yielded to me out of pity
—sheer self-pity, in fact—and so have *become* her own portrait, if Belcredi hadn't seen the danger and sharpened his in-
sinuations? And, yes, if I hadn't then seized upon Frida as *my*
timeless image—instead of that . . . sentimental whore.

Whom I gladly would have left to my slippery antagonist.
Ah, Pietro Damiani! (*An invisible Belcredi is at his side.*)
"Was it not perhaps you who started that obscene rumor that
my holy mother had illicit relations with the Bishop of Au-
gusta?" Belcredi has too often been underestimated—written
off as the empty vehicle for the actor who plays him. But you
can glimpse his self-awareness in those analyses he offered of
me as I was twenty years ago, for what could he do but read
me through his own experience of that "immediate lucidity
which comes from acting?" A lucidity, he said, that at once
put me out of key with my own feelings, which seemed to me
not exactly false, but like something I was obliged to give the
value then and there of—what did he say?—an act of intelli-
gence, to make up for that sincere cordial warmth which I felt
lacking. And so, he said, I exaggerated, let myself go, appeared
inconstant, fatuous, even ridiculous. Well put, and with unusual loquacity. For if Belcredi was my secret double—as who
was not, in this play of mirrors that has multiplied a single
predicament?—he most often cast himself as my laconic opposite. The master of the offhand slur, the strategic silence. Yes,
and working deviously here before your eyes, just as twenty
years ago, to prevent the hysteria of the Marchioness from
sweeping her into the past with me. Ah, Damiani, "I am grate-

ful to you, believe me, I am grateful to you for the hindrance you put in my way."

Did you see him, near the end, trying to stare me down with that look of false surprise when I spoke of those who had ridden behind me and had pricked my horse until it reared and threw me to the ground? He risked no words, but that slight twitch in the cheek betrayed the thrust. And when I said to the Marchioness, "It doesn't matter who it was"—ah, to see his face then, as he measured the generosity, the contempt, and the threat! But words did come, as you heard. When in the sweet exhilaration of their fear I swept Frida into my arms (*miming the scene now with relish*) and forced him to raise his hands against me, you heard him cry out: "You're not a madman!" Not mad, eh! One step to Landolph's side, a quick draw, a thrust into the guts—and again that cry: "He's not mad! He's not mad!" (*Laughing in bitter satisfaction.*) As Belcredi thought he well knew, for his own guilt cried out in those words of attempted revenge upon his . . . just executioner.

Useless words, of course (*fixing us again with his eyes*)— or at least superfluous. How could they condemn me to this solitude, where I have always been? Shall we confess the truth? In trying to play our own roles in full consciousness, we can never escape from the self-isolating madness of role-playing. We only invite the subtler madness of the role-behind-the-role. For every "I" is a comic mistake and a murderous trap— even that "I" who earlier this evening said with such confidence to the others, "I'm only sorry for you that have to live your madness so agitatedly without knowing and seeing it." Even *this* "I" who now tries, after the main performance, to confess the truth. Yes, and even the "I" just behind this "I"—for the regression is endless—who calls himself Luigi Pirandello, and who says to us all (*removing his robe and tossing it to the floor, disclosing a black business suit of the 1920's*): "My friend, when someone lives, he lives and does not watch himself. Well, arrange things so he does watch himself in the act of living, a prey to his passions, by placing a mirror before him (*removing coronet and wig, so that the red and white face is now adorned by a distinguished head of dark hair, greying at the temples*):

either he will be astonished and dismayed by his own appearance and turn his eyes away so as not to see himself, or he will spit at his image in disgust, or will angrily thrust out his fist to smash it—"

PLAYER QUEEN (*a hoarsely masculine voice in the darkness, downstage right*):

That'll do now. It's time.

PLAYER KING (*speeding up*):

"If he was weeping he will no longer be able to do so, if he was laughing he will no longer be able to laugh. In short, there will be some manifestation of pain. This manifestation of pain is my theater."

PLAYER QUEEN:

Words!

PLAYER KING (*still addressing us*):

Yes, words! (*He draws from his coat pocket a book, flips the pages, and reads.*) Words that are "the action spoken," words "not invented but . . . born when an author is truly identified with his creature to the point of feeling it as he feels himself, desiring it as it desires itself—"

PLAYER QUEEN (*as a spot now discloses her seated in an armchair, a severe-looking figure in a black tailored suit, watching a closed-circuit screen on which the* PLAYER KING *is visible*):

Make it snappy. *Who* is truly identified?

PLAYER KING (*flipping pages, then reading—to us and, on the screen, to the* PLAYER QUEEN—*with increasing insistence*):

"I . . . have no conception of what I am and have always refrained from finding out for fear of offending all the life which continually seethes within me—"

PLAYER QUEEN (*laughing*):

Refrained? Through all these agitated words?

PLAYER KING (*almost shouting his text*):

"A man, I have tried to tell something of myself to other men, without any ambition—"

PLAYER QUEEN:

Come now, it's late.

PLAYER KING:

"—except perhaps of avenging myself for having been born. And yet (*now burlesquing his own lines*) life, in spite of all that it has made me suffer, is so beautiful! (And here is another positive statement without even a shadow of logic, and yet so true and deeply felt—"

PLAYER QUEEN:

Finished or not— (*she flips a switch, blacking out both the screen and the spot on the* PLAYER KING, *then turns to us—a taut smile on the heavy features of the actor who plays her.*) So true, so deeply felt! Shouldn't he enter the Nomenclature at once? Call it the Grievance Game. Or better, the Studio of Art. *That* will stop those earnest critics from saying that no one plays at being an Artist in my house of illusions. To play Pirandello in Studio 39 is to use theater as my Chief of Police uses politics: as a way of penetrating into the reality that the game offers us. And if not always with such masculine address, then backwards—like my feverish Judge who so loves to crawl. What shivering satisfaction for a King—to suffer suicide, over and over again, by thrusting a borrowed sword into an imagined double! And what ecstasy to be the real sufferer of that pain of being fake, to see the grotesque comedy of that suffering, and to feel the pain of that comedy! To be all of this seething life and yet nothing at all—a real unreal *me* whose image, like that of the Chief of Police in the Mausoleum Studio—or General Franco in the Valley of the Fallen—will be reflected to infinity!

Because any number can be persuaded to play, each with his own scenario.

Of course, if you take in the whirl at a glance, the game may seem to be up. How can a fake self manage to suffer? Who feels the pain of my non-existence? But no Pirandellian script allows that perception for long. A moment later we'll be undeniably *there*, like that anguished Father in *Six Characters*, realer than real, to experience our betrayal and our impossibility. And why not? It's what we want at bottom: not to be absent but to feel ourselves speeding again toward Absence. What drives the cycles of sex, religion, and revolution but that ache for the hard and massy Image which will make us what we already suspect ourselves of being: a dream of potency, an impotent reflection—in short, the living power of death? And what *can* be meant by those who say, "It is impossible to make against art . . . the sort of case Genet has been forging against the Other and which he will finally use to trap us all"? There is no Other in this house. We are here together. And this Establishment itself is the House of Art. If the Grand Balcony hasn't needed a studio for Pirandellos, that's because a more knowledgeable artist stands here before you. (*She rises, turns, and approaches the rear mirror-wall, enabling her reflection to address us.*)

Call me Madame Irma, if you want—but I'm no such person. Nor will I bore you with a striptease of the kind that thrills our rhetorical King. It's enough to say, "As Queen of our revels, I am absent in this presence" (*gesturing toward her own appearance*). For though in the last two scenes of *The Balcony* Irma always becomes the image of a real Queen, she herself is already played by one who is "unfindable," as the Envoy likes to put it—one who has attained a "threatened invisibility." If it's true that no one here plays at being an Artist, I must be she. But whatever may be imagined in certain studios, we don't merely suffer our destiny here with the neurotic retrospection exhibited by our King. We approach it as fast as we can. Our power and profit lie in being what we are not and in not being what we are—if I may steal a phrase from a philosopher who knows how to use words to canonize a criminal. After all (*fac-*

ing us again), he who plays King is a pitiful nonentity, impris-
oning himself in a theatrical world from which there is but one
paradoxical exit: the act of making that prison into the house
of pleasure that it has always secretly been. To acknowledge
our royal calling, to become Queen (*seating herself again with
a smile*), is to exploit our condition as servants of love—to
lose ourselves in the Image.

In that act of truth you participate, according to your tastes
and abilities, whenever you visit this house. What's your daily
life compared with that? An awkward fumbling in the dark.
And if some outside these walls describe our play as fantasy,
that's because they haven't yet recognized their parts. Every
revolution is already contained by the Establishment. Icono-
clasts pursue their own images of breaking. Together, as our
play shows, we penetrate into the providential fixity.

In a few minutes, when this set plunges into the wings, you
will begin to witness the generation of images. First that of a
Bishop, more real than any who holds office, approaching the
goal of all hierarchy: the transubstantiation of function into a
mode of being. A necessary blasphemy. No function can attain
its end except through negation. Nor could the episcopal function itself be imagined without that penitent who arouses so
ambiguous a desire. Then on to the images of Judge and General—who will be almost interchangeable with the thief and the
ridden mare from which they emanate. All speeding toward
a death that you'll hear in the spurts of machine-gun fire ejacu-
lated at the climax of each scene. But then who takes the stage?
Yourselves: so tenderly accepting your role before the three
mirrors that give you back—with impotent age, torn gloves,
artificial flowers, and . . . yes, the lice. For would you be here
at all, the willing fundament of hierarchy, if you didn't love
the whip?

After those four studio-glimpses, you'll want to peek behind
the scenes into this room—from which, as the unmade bed reflected in the studio mirrors will have testified, you have already
been watching the play. Reality now. The reality of those who
live prudently if precariously within this house of illusions. For
we too can be seduced by our images—whether we're loyal

like Carmen, who dreams herself the Immaculate Conception in front of that kneeling bank clerk, or treacherous like Chantal, who escapes to arouse the blood of those who imagine they attack us. Even Irma is hardly immune—as you'll see when I tell Carmen how I sometimes repeat to myself, in silence, "You're a bawd, a boss of a whorehouse," and everything flies off— "studios, girls, crystals, laces, balconies, everything takes it on the lam, rises up and carries me off!" But it's not in the telling. A moment of unspeakable fullness, there, face to face with Carmen in the studio of studios. Compared to that, my game with the Chief of Police and Arthur is just a tired replay of old emotions, the friction of habit.

But at the end of this scene a shot will enter my room, shatter a mirror, and make Arthur—"my body," I will have just said, ". . . but set beside me"—into the corpse he intended to play. In that moment even my own jewels—my rocks, the only things I have that are real—will seem threatened. And with death will come the Envoy of Absence. But as I prepare to re-ceive him, you must turn to what you still imagine the most real scene of all—the theater of operations outside the Grand Balcony, where Chantal is embracing that serious plumber who belongs to the partisans' Andromeda network. Andromeda! They're already flying high, as the Chief will have said. But am I their Medusa? No: they freeze themselves—like Chantal and her Perseus, Roger and his Angélique, locked in each other's arms for a moment of farewell, watched over by you and the men with guns. Their revolutionary aubade, with its well-rehearsed lines, makes its own studio. Singing, as Roger says, is the last resort. (And he's right. Even in speaking to you, I have to fight off the cadences—trying to keep it cool.) Chantal, of course, must become the Pasionara of our civil war, and she'll be shot on the balcony in Scene 8. And her revolutionary prig, after selling her for a dream of victory, must rush off to-ward *his* still hidden destiny.

Now, having seen the reality of illusion and the illusion of reality, you'll be ready to take in the end. Three scenes of undoing. First the ruins of the Funeral Studio—because the theater of death itself must die into life-beyond-death, where

the Envoy poses riddles of Absence and recruits new blood for
the Figures, where the Chief of Police still yearns for his fixity,
and where I—after putting up some tough resistance, for I won
my spurs with the troops—approach my destiny as Queen.
Then the balcony itself, where we mime the rites of all power.
We are dead! Long live the Image! And at last, back in my
room, we enter the vortex of Absence.

It gets tricky here. You must keep your eyes open if you
want, like the Chief, to keep vigil over your entire death—
because that's what we're up to. "A true image," the Envoy
will say, "born of a false spectacle." We begin with a comic
whirl. Bishop, Judge, and General—their roles now their lives,
their studio the nation—act as you can predict. But when they
find their power play blocked, they want to withdraw to the
absolute and impotent dignity that once had been theirs. Like
the revolution itself, which has made it as a wonderful failure,
the whole business is starting over again. Because it's always
the illusion *beyond* the reality of illusion that we want. But not
yet. Not without the heroic whirl. Lined up before my screens,
we'll spy on the Mausoleum Studio, where Roger, dressed like
the Chief of Police, plays out his role as Hero to the limits of its
destiny. And as we watch, the mirror at the back of my room
will part—thanks to the craft of a Queen behind this Queen—
(*gesturing toward the mirror-wall behind her which at this
moment does begin slowly to open*) so that you too can see
the meaning of all revolution. (*In the darkness behind the
mirror we barely make out a seated and shrouded figure.*)
When Roger places his foot on the slave, I hope you recognize
yourself from Scene 4. And when he proclaims, "My history
was lived so that a glorious page might be written and then
read. It's reading that counts,' remember that the Envoy had
repeated those words to me. The lesson's well learned. And
when Roger then takes the knife and makes the gesture of
castration, won't it be well played, as the Chief will say? So
well that now it's *his* turn. Having seen his own image, "stronger
than strong, deader than dead," the Chief must slowly walk
backward through the mirror into this tomb, where he'll sit for
two thousand years as his role perfects itself in our minds. (*Be-*

hind the mirror, a spot begins slowly to come up on the
SACRIFICED PAWN, *seated in an armchair on casters, wearing a*
dressing-gown, toque, and thick socks, his face covered with a
blood-stained handkerchief.) The machine-guns start firing
again.

And I? "The Queen attains her reality when she withdraws,
absents herself, or dies." So what can I do (*rising from her*
chair) but dismiss the other Figures, begin to turn out the
lights (*signalling to the wing for her own spot to begin going*
down), tell the Envoy to call me Madame Irma, and then send
him—and you—home from this studio of your pleasure? "All
these performances so that I can remain alone. . . ." (*Smiling.*)
It's an act of will, you may be certain. Read *Our Lady of the*
Flowers. A "vision of the world obtained by an effort, sometimes exhausting, of the taut, buttressed will." But isn't it
worth the price? So put out the lights. "In a little while," I
will say, "I'll have to start all over again."
(*Spot out on the* PLAYER QUEEN.)

SACRIFICED PAWN (*wearily, without removing his veronica*):

"Finished, it's finished, nearly finished, it must be nearly fin-
ished."
(*Pause.*)
Time? "The same as usual." Place? "There's nowhere else."
Action? "Old endgame lost of old. . . ." Theme?
(*With fervor.*)
"Ah the old questions, the old answers, there's nothing like
them!"
(*Yawns.*)
No need to rush toward absence. No one here to be nameless.
"Absent, always. It all happened without me."
(*Pause.*)
Then what's taking its course? A stalemate in too many moves.
Hamm's bad dreams in a nutshell.
(*Pause.*)
"Me to play." No others? "But where would I find them?" And
the dialogue? ". . . babble, babble, words, like the solitary child

who turns himself into children, two, three, so as to be to-
gether, and whisper together, in the dark."
(Brief laugh.)
"Can there be misery . . . loftier than mine?" Ask that madman
who thought the end of the world had come. Outside the win-
dow: ashes. And inside?
(Pause.)
Infinite space. "If I can hold my peace, and sit quiet"—tell
Pascal.
(Pause.)
Eliot, too. "The end is in the beginning and yet you go on."
(Pause.)
And where were you when it all began?
(Narrative tone.)
It was a dull day, I remember, twenty-four by the clock, when
you sat in the last row of the theater, tired of playwrights who
pretend to be able.
(Pause. Normal tone.)
Nothing doing.
(Pause. Narrative tone.)
It was a bright night, I remember, zero by the telescope in
every direction, when the theater came alive in your words.
Aha, you said. Four-dimensional chess? On the board, in the
shelter, on the boards, in your head. The objective? To pretend
to continue to begin to end. Every move a loss. A leap. A repe-
tition? A design.
(Pause. Normal tone.)
A bit forced, that. Try it again?
(Pause.)
No, our revels are ended. I've thrown away the dog and the gaff.
(Anxiously.)
"We're not beginning to . . . to . . . mean something?"
(Brief laugh.)
More like nothing. But for them?
(Tonelessly.)
They said to us, Don't you see, night is dark, day is light, out-
side is there, inside is here, the past is gone, the future is coming?

They said to us, It's only common sense, bodies aren't minds, we aren't you, objects aren't void, the void is no object. They said to us, Wake up—how can desire be fear, and love hate, and grief joy? Come out of it—you're only invented!
(Laughs. Tonelessly.)
But we say to ourselves—sometimes, No, we don't see, our eyes have gone white, it's light black here, and it's always now. We say to ourselves—sometimes, it's no secret, those windows are eyes, this skull's a shelter, we're all in your mind, and I'm telling the story.
(Violently.)
You know who killed Mother Pegg! And if it's not true that we love each other as we hate ourselves, why do you laugh?
(Wearily.)
Is your order less cluttered? Your clutter less empty?
(Pause.)
What life isn't death?
(Pause.)
"Since that's the way we're playing it . . ."
(He reaches for the handkerchief, decides otherwise, returns his hand to his lap.)
". . . let's play it that way . . . ."
(Brief tableau. Spot down; houselights up. The scattering of uncertain applause is interrupted by a disturbance in the fourth row as someone presses awkwardly to the aisle.)

WITNESS:

But how can you stop now? Is that the whole show?
(Indignant murmurs. A few shouts: "Sit down!" "Split!" All three spots come up, catching the players in some disarray. They glance at each other, then turn upon the nondescript character who has now reached the apron.)

FIRST PLAYER *(reaching for his sword)*:

Strip him. Who are *you*?

SECOND PLAYER *(removing his wig)*:

No, seduce him. What's your game?

THIRD PLAYER *(elaborately blowing his nose)*:

Old stuff. Bottle him.

WITNESS *(who persists in facing the stage)*:

It's better already—conversation! What made you think a single character could speak for a play? Have you been reading Kenneth Burke on *Julius Caesar*?

FIRST PLAYER:

If Pirandello is right, who isn't a character?

SECOND PLAYER:

And if the character is a mask for the absence of the playwright—

THIRD PLAYER:

—a play is already a monologue.

WITNESS:

It won't do, my friends. The plays also include *us*.

FIRST PLAYER:

As we explained.

WITNESS:

You explained only how they *pretend* to include us.

SECOND PLAYER:

Playing *is* pretending.

WITNESS:

If the cast of *The Balcony* believed its own account of the pretense, the performance would be a chaotic dream—unscripted theater by an apostle of Artaud. No. Whatever their truth, these plays are lying mirrors of their own playing.

THIRD PLAYER:

Of course! Why else did we let Genet defate Pirandello and Beckett annihilate Genet? Did you miss the irony, or are you trying to give Pirandello the last word? *Tonight We Improvise* is out of date. Say something new or sit down.

WITNESS:

What's new? The old questions, the old answers, which we have to keep on translating. Your aggressive monologues remain caught in the irony these plays *contain*. What is it that so delightedly attacks the inauthenticity, perversity, or absence of the ego? Of course: the ego. The so-called crisis of the "self" in the theater since Ibsen is like approaching the great doubt-block in Zen. The entire will is focused on the task of annihilating the will. Result? Deadlock, in which we experience the ego as the living contradiction that it is. That's the situation we're *playing* here. Pirandello, Genet, and Beckett don't directly undo the "self"—even though that seems to be what's happening on stage. They variously invite us to play "winding it up tight"— which reveals the absurdity of everything except letting go.

SECOND PLAYER:

Zen, yet! Is that what you're high on? You want the Dojo Studio?

WITNESS:

We could do worse. To *play* Zen might be to undo the willful Japanese discipline and return to Tao. And if *you* want a French antidote to Genet, read Jacques Copeau. He knew enough about Diderot's and Pirandello's paradoxes, and his *Notes sur le métier de comédien* recognize that a player needs not a taut and deceptive will but just the opposite: a difficult decontraction of the self, a silent openness to the given. What happens when we are momentarily undone by such play? No longer identifying with a reified "self," the "I" becomes no more than a participatory presence attentive to the actual. Though Pirandello, Genet, and Beckett don't explicitly teach that discipline and in fact seem to deny it, their plays invite and require it no less than do Shakespeare's or Molière's, Ibsen's or Lorca's. Copeau recognized this when he composed his own somewhat Pirandellian script, *L'Illusion*, for his young troupe in Bourgogne: he let the actors present themselves in a playing that was ambiguously fiction and truth, life and dream, but that moved toward a celebration of the freshness that may be re-born in us during the moment of attention when we are stripped, when we have become "nothing.' (*To the* FIRST PLAYER.) Without such moments of alert availability could you have found the self-entrapping action of that man who so very differently plays Henry IV? Could you have worked out the gracefully grotesque movements that would clarify and heighten that action? And could you have joined others to compose from the rhythms of baffled opposition implied in the script a tragi-comic dance of masks?

FIRST PLAYER:

The play doesn't show *us* as trapped by role-playing?

WITNESS:

How could it? In and through these plays we show ourselves how the *ego* is trapped. In *Henry IV* by rage against its own inauthenticity. In *The Balcony* by lust for the power exerted by that inauthenticity. And in *Endgame*—

THIRD PLAYER:

Wait a minute! Who isn't the ego? If the man playing Henry IV saw how his rage becomes a prison, he'd be enraged by *that*— as Pirandello clearly was. Irma understands very well that we're imprisoned by lust for the image—and can only profit from the inevitable. And the consciousness that plays Hamm knows to the bone that consciousness is its own jailer—hates it, loves it, goes on playing it, because it *is* that. The ultimate prison is self-consciousness. And seeing that helps nobody.

WITNESS:

Only "nobody" can see and be helped. But as soon as "nobody" *has* seen, the ego claims to be somebody again—no longer nameless but "the man who knows how to play Henry IV," or Pirandello, or a Queen, or a Hamm. Not just a witness or an actor but an *agent*. A new identity shapes itself out of the identity-destroying insight. Somebody takes action, if only to demonstrate the superiority of his knowledge.

SECOND PLAYER:

You are describing yourself?

WITNESS:

Insofar as I pretend to be somebody.

THIRD PLAYER *(violently)*:

"Use your head, can't you, use your head, you're on earth, there's no cure for that!" I *am* self-consciousness.

WITNESS:

Gabriel Marcel once said, "If we begin, like Descartes, by assuming that my essence is self-consciousness, there is no longer a way out." The performed action of *Endgame* begins right there. But our action of performance, which unfolds the predicament of the characters with such lovely stylized comedy in an open world, tacitly recognizes that as players we're prior to self-consciousness. That's why we're fundamentally nobody —and why an attentive playing of these scripts shows them to be remarkable forms of lying truth. Each presents a world within which the play itself couldn't be presented.

FIRST PLAYER:

Henry IV couldn't be presented within its own world? But Pirandello obviously thought it could. What about *Six Characters* or *Each in His Own Way*?

WITNESS:

Sleight-of-hand. Mirror tricks. Pirandello liked to tempt us with illusions of an endless regression, even while contradicting them. But just as no statement can adequately formulate the act of speech that founds and includes it, no performed action can mirror its founding performance. As participants in a given field of play, however, we can mediate analogically between those two levels. In *Henry IV* we do share the characters' objective: to cope with the madness of unconscious role-playing by deliberately playing our own roles. But for each character that objective means a self-isolating attempt to cope with the madness of others. And for us it means a collaborative exploration of our own potential madness. To play *Henry IV* is neither to impose an "identity" nor to regret its loss. Opening ourselves to the roles, and so loosening our own mistaken identifications, we learn the tragicomedy of our usual insistence on being somebody. If presented by characters within its own world, *Henry IV* would at once become a function of their conscious or unconscious aggression and its style would therefore be transformed. It could no longer be our grotesque and pseudo-realistic *commedia*, our self-liberating dance of masks through which we discover that the search for solidity is finally an irrelevant problem.

FIRST PLAYER:

But even for us there's only role-playing!

WITNESS:

Who wants anything else—and why? A "real face" is another mask. Playing is no enraging trap. Nor is it fundamentally what Michael Goldman in *The Actor's Freedom* calls a venture in "sustained ego-protection." No doubt in its incomplete forms, playing can enable individuals to assimilate and so withstand a threatening reality, but finally it directs our attention toward its intersubjective ground—with respect to which all ego-protection is resistance or evasion. The freedom of actors and witnesses can't be described in terms of any ego-psychology with its "universe of satisfactions." That freedom is a condition of detachment made possible by a continually reaffirmed act of attention and consent, through which we engage in a spontaneous dialogue with the actual. Because no role can ever be "mine" or exhaust "what we are," and because "what we are" sustains our reciprocal play, the phrase that opened your monologue is finally no prison sentence. "Here we are . . . together . . . forever." Yes. In the *Bhagavad-Gita* the man who learns to play the warrior is told in effect by the Nobody who plays

his charioteer: "We are here together not only in this moment
but forever."

SECOND PLAYER:

Perversity! You turn skepticism into faith, West into East,
nothing into everything.

WITNESS:

Not I but the fields of play, as you can see if you attend to our
playing.

SECOND PLAYER:

Not in *The Balcony*. Its doctrine is the reverse of yours.

WITNESS:

Let's agree that *The Balcony* is a brilliant demonstration of
why we are almost always ruled by more or less cultivated
gangsters. A true image born of a false spectacle. We seek
illusion. Why? To escape from fear. The real subject of *The
Balcony* is fear of death in all its forms.

SECOND PLAYER:

Lust for death, perhaps—

WITNESS:

Not for death but for a theatrical Absence, which hides a fear
of the anonymity that is the necessary condition of Presence.
What is that "taut, buttressed will" opposing? Oblivion. That's
why in the style of *The Balcony* every act of darkness must be
garishly lit and mirrored. Aware of its nothingness, the ego
wants to spy on everything, keep vigil over its entire death,
avoid any loss of self-consciousness, see itself reflected to infinity. And *The Balcony* understands very well the central place
of that murderous desire in our culture. But we can realize the
truth of that understanding only through a playing that undoes
the falsity of the spectacle. The characters in *The Balcony*, in-
dulging real impulses within an ambiguously real or fake *mise-
en-scène*, seek a fictive absence that can serve as a powerful

mask for an anxiously impotent ego. But as we explore the meaning of that search through the spectacular style that transforms—especially in the play's final version, on which you based your monologue—even the revolutionary movement outside the brothel into a symbolic tableau, we are neither seeking the characters' gratification nor merely exposing it in the manner that Irma's final speech suggests. Despite the fact that *The Balcony* ostensibly reverses the thesis of Rotrou's *Véritable Saint Genest*—for it shows not that the theater leads to the altar but that the altar is already theater—our performance here is no speeding toward Absence but a mutual participation that is a sign of Presence.

SECOND PLAYER:

I refuse to believe that.

THIRD PLAYER:

And I *can't* believe it. *Endgame* is founded on self-isolating doubt.

WITNESS:

The performed action is—no doubt. But not the action of performance, which implicitly agrees with Unamuno that the "methodical doubt of Descartes is a comic doubt . . . the doubt of a man who acts as if he doubted without ever doubting."

THIRD PLAYER:

But a serious predicament can be painfully comic. The stage here, as Tom Driver said, is "a model of consciousness, which if it creates order, does so only to discover that order has no ontological ground." *Endgame* calls in question every necessary distinction of thought. Is Hamm a mind, a person, a role, a piece of meat? Is he blind or can he see the whiteness of his own eyes? Is anyone outside the shelter or not? Has guilt increased solitude or has solitude produced fantasies of guilt? Could Clov ever leave—or is he part of Hamm or just another piece on the board? Could anyone ever "be there better than that?" Unanswerable questions—these and others. Dead end.

We can only replay the endgame. That's the meaning of our doubtful absence.

WITNESS:

The meaning of *my* doubtful absence and *our* playful presence. True enough, we can only pretend to continue to begin to end. But if, for the masks within the play, that objective is the trap of the "I," for us it's an open field. We don't need to establish any of the distinctions of dualistic common sense or systematic thought. I may be a figment of your imagination, or you of mine—or both of us may be *personae* in a play that can never become our object. Why fuss? Only because somebody wants to possess himself and his world. Each center of consciousness in *Endgame*'s performed action—from Nagg with his biscuits of sentiment, through Clov with his ten-by-ten kitchen, to Hamm with his nihilistic paradoxes—tries to turn our field into an object. That's the meaning of *Endgame*'s style. Every no-thing is rigorously and comically reduced to a possessed loss. But in the action of performance we let the field of non-duality be what it is: the ground of our reciprocal play. And we experience the fact that corrosive doubt isn't finally an intellectual problem at all. "The metaphysical origins of pessimism," as Marcel said in *Being and Having*, "are the same as the origins of non-disposability." Pessimism results from saying, "I am my life." In playing the masks who say that and so condemn themselves to doubtful absence, we enact a different saying: "In this life we lose ourselves." And that participation is, for us, the meaning of pretending to continue to begin to end. The "I" is indeed a lost game. As Didi and Gogo had already said, "Nothing to be done." In variously playing that game, in learning to do nothing, we find what plays us.

FIRST PLAYER:

If so, who are you?

WITNESS:

For myself, no one.

SECOND PLAYER:

Then who speaks through the mask?

WITNESS:

Perhaps you? Who understands is already speaking.

THIRD PLAYER:

To himself—who is no one.

WITNESS:

With us—who may be unnameable.

FIRST PLAYER:

I still don't understand.

SECOND PLAYER:

And I refuse to believe it.

THIRD PLAYER:

And I doubt it.

WITNESS:

Fortunately it's never up to "me." How is it possible for those who play this very script to hear and speak our words? If they so much as ask that question, they have entered our circle, are with us here and now, and are open to such light as we may have. And if so (*he turns to us, as the theater disappears and we find ourselves holding a book in our hands*), you already know how to take part in three plays—*The Caucasian Chalk Circle, Murder in the Cathedral,* and *The Tower*—which understand these matters better than any "I" can do.

SEVEN

BEARING
WITNESS

X: Let's hope so. As actors and witnesses become the play, so readers become the book. Can we take it from here?

Y: Show how these plays, though not necessarily more powerful than those of Pirandello, Genet, and Beckett, do allow the performed action to unfold the anonymous Yes that's implicit in our medium? But where to begin?

Z: Perhaps with the fact that in each the playwright has reaffirmed the dramatic tradition. Hofmannsthal in the twenties could express his political pessimism by rewriting Calderón. Eliot in the thirties could expound a martyrdom by drawing on *Everyman* and Aeschylean tragedy. And Brecht in the forties could elaborate a Marxist moral through Oriental narrative theater and Shakespearean festive comedy. No signs there of a dead end.

Y: But you talk as if *The Tower, Murder in the Cathedral*, and *The Caucasion Chalk Circle* were merely past attempts to express ideas. Do we need one more historical account of their allegorical meaning? That won't help us engage the forms of our present playing.

X: Why not begin with the fact that each playwright has passed through the crisis that continued to obsess Pirandello, Genet, and Beckett? Hofmannsthal's first play, *Gestern*, broached the problem he would later develop in the "Letter of Lord Chandos": "Actions are impotent, and words are empty." In Brecht's first play, *Baal*, the protagonist shares that predicament and wants to feed on his own death, his own rich nothingness. And the protagonist of Eliot's first play, *Sweeney Agonistes*, knows that speech can't express the horror of his meaningless world: "But I've gotta use words when I talk to you." Baal and Sweeney are among the ancestors of Hamm. But Hofmannsthal, Brecht, and Eliot were able to move beyond such nihilism toward an aesthetic of gesture that implies the possibility of finding authenticity through giving ourselves to the field of play.

Y: In Eliot's later plays, as in Hofmannsthal's *Difficult Man*, even the brittle conventions of drawing-room comedy allow gestures of self-abandonment. But you still talk like a historian.

Z: And a bad one. You ignore all the ideological and formal differences. Hofmannsthal's symbolic gestures purport to disclose the universal. Eliot's thinly verbal gestures are little more than vehicles for Christian doctrine. And Brecht understood a *gestus* to be neither symbolic nor verbal but a concrete demonstration of a socially significant attitude within a dialectical situation.

X: But I want to point beyond those differences toward something quite central. In his "Prologue" to Brecht's *Baal*, Hofmannsthal called the protean actor himself the "symbolic man." Now don't *The Tower, Murder in the Cathedral*, and *The Caucasian Chalk Circle* show us this man, who is so vulnerable to the tyranny of the mask, being drawn toward his true end? In each, the actor-protagonist learns to bear witness.

Z: You think Azdak is a martyr, like Becket or Sigismund? Not likely. And what about the real protagonist of Brecht's play? Is Grusha an actor?

X: She is, in her own way—and I shouldn't ignore her. Each of these four characters explores a different histrionic range. Sigismund, beginning in the paradoxical innocence of a feral nobility, moves swiftly through the life-roles offered him toward the ripeness of his self-abandonment. Becket, who is already trapped in clerical self-deception, must see himself truly before he can learn not to act or suffer. Azdak, who at first seems fixed within his cowardly cleverness, and Grusha, who seems limited to a peasant shrewdness, must both receive an elaborate education in role-playing as they respond to what the Singer calls the terrible temptation to do good. Finally, all four are drawn toward a disarming transparency of gesture, a non-acting action, that points to the field of mutuality without which our playing would be impossible.

Z: That's much too glib a reduction of three very different ideological structures.

Y: At least it is too narrow a description of our three ways of playing. After all, none of these scripts pretends to locate its meanings exclusively in its world of characters. Two are festival plays; one is a miming of such a play. As community events, they speak *with* us, through our action of performance. Mustn't we therefore understand the symbolic actions and tableaux of *The Tower*, the quasi-liturgical sequences of *Murder in the Cathedral*, and the demonstrations and songs of *The Caucasian Chalk Circle* as shared gestures that lead us toward some analogous witnessing?

Z: You sound like another Jacques Copeau, dreaming of some theater that might come into being "when the man in the audience murmurs in his heart and with his heart the same words spoken by the man on the stage." But no modern play can be a rite. Even *Murder in the Cathedral* contains a dialectical complexity that should bring to the audience some surprise and discomfort.

X: True enough. Each of these plays grants that the idea of "community" is now radically problematic. If the action recognizes our grounding unity, it must also admit that we exist as self-conscious modern individuals only by denying that recognition.

Z: That's a loaded way of putting it.

X: The dramatic medium is hardly neutral.

Y: Can we suspend our differences long enough to find out whether each of these plays does consist of some shared action or spectrum of movements through which characters, actors, and spectators approach a common witnessing?

X: Then we'll have to curb our lust for ideology. We must assume that Hofmannsthal's apocalyptic Neoplatonism, Eliot's Anglo-Catholicism, and Brecht's evasive Marxism are dramatic constructs, no more important than the roles in the play—or than our own rigid selves.

Z: What? The playwrights wouldn't accept that assumption for one moment.

X: They knew well enough, in their different ways, that ideas are always the relative and provisional utterances of transient *personae*—and that the ego exists only to abandon itself. "To act," Hofmannsthal said in *Ad me ipsum*, "is to give oneself up."

Y: In *The Elder Statesman*, Lord Calverton says:

"I've been freed from the self that pretends to be someone;
And becoming no one, I begin to live."

Z: You want me to quote from *The Measures Taken*?

X: Why be doctrinaire? Think of *Mother Courage*. What about a mute gesture like Kattrin's drumming on the roof to save the children?

Z: But Brecht never simply endorsed such non-ideological self-sacrifice. He remained as much a trimmer on that question, and on most others, as Mother Courage or Galileo or the Good Person of Setzuan.

Y: In short, his ideas remained provisional, histrionic, appropriate to the dialectical situation. Remember your own warning about the *gestus*. And what if a playwright should posthumously object to our considering his ideas as dramatic constructs? We'd simply have to retort that he has already abandoned himself to the play, where the forms of our acting and witnessing speak more cogently than any discursive rhetoric.

Z: If so, why must we indulge in all this talk? "Actual plays," Brecht said, "can be understood only in performance." Shall we adjourn to the theater?

Y: Maybe we should. John Russell Brown once remarked that the best dramatic criticism takes place in the rehearsal room. And it's not likely that our dialogue could make explicit the responses we might share in the simplest dramatic event. We're much too quick to translate our perceptions into defensive and mutually exclusive assertions.

X: But why give up so soon? We aren't fixed types like the speakers in Brecht's *Messingkauf Dialogues*. Can't we each confess to at least as much indeterminacy as we can hear in the

Brechtian voice that informs those dialogues? If so, why not join to risk a multi-dimensional speech that might render some of our shared or sharable responses?

Y: Reconstitute our self-torn body—through a fiction?

Z: We'd need three fictions, one for each of the problematic communities that these plays invite us to become.

X: Then let it be three. Shall we begin with *The Tower*?

Y: Can't we break this habit of chronological thinking? It always leads to some historicist conclusion that was really implicit in the method. And each of these plays already reverses or transcends time—for its own good reasons.

Z: Even a perspective on history, of course, is always a present perspective. *Chalk Circle* might work for a start: it includes a dialectical invitation to enter the circle of play.

Y: And we could then move to *Murder*, which understands that our participation in history must always be a celebration here and now.

X: And then to *The Tower*, which invites us to see the end of our histrionic dream. Can we manage a fiction of that waking to light?

Z: A baroque approach, at least.

Y: And let *our* readers take it from there.

~~~~~~~~~~~

Entering

the circle of play is finding that somehow we're already there. Brecht claimed to have written his spare and utilitarian "learning-plays" for the performers. And though *The Caucasian Chalk Circle* is no such play— being a theatrical spectacle of Shakespearean variety—Brecht wrote it too for the performers: it requires those of us who think ourselves spectators to move, step by step, toward the discovery that we are participants. We begin with an embarrassingly simple Prologue, a utopian fantasy so far from the conditions of our action of performance that

"Learning-plays . . . plays which are instructive for the performers. They need no audience."
—Brecht

"Theater is a stupid

the ironic discrepancies threaten to explode the play before it has begun. But then, folding back on itself, the Prologue leads us into a subtler participation than its editorializing peasants could understand. It's an old pastoral strategy: the simple will contain the complex. As attentive spectators, we're already open to the claims of justice—and eager to share in a more complex playing. Aware of it or not, we have already entered two of the play's concentric circles and are proceeding toward their hidden center. That's the movement we will here act and witness. *The Caucasian Chalk Circle* will be for us, as for the roles we play, a field of convergence that draws "actors" and "witnesses" toward a realization of our reciprocal identity. No Brechtian alienation effects? *Verfremden* means to make strange. And as Brecht understood with Viktor Shklovsky, "making strange" refreshes the attention. In this play every apparent "distancing" will make possible a more intimately critical participation, not a hypnotic "identification" with the roles but a more complete sharing in our present action of performance. And what's our shared objective? Like the main roles, we want "to see justice done," or "to join the action," or "to play the golden age." However we phrase it, each will imply the others—just as each of *us* finally implies the others. Like this:

simplicity, if it is not shrewdly complex."
—Brecht

"Often the songs are interpreted as 'alienation-effects.' . . . But Brecht wanted the actors, during Grusha's reunion with her fiancé, to mime most exactly the text of the Chorus. . . . The song as poetic expression of silence. And when expressing Simon Chachava's reproachful thoughts, the Singer should not here, as on other occasions, sing as though apart from the action, telling a tale, but angrily, accusingly."
—Angelika Hurwicz

HAVING SURVIVED THE WAR, WE PLAY THE SEARCH FOR JUSTICE
    A bare stage. Evenly and coolly lit. Canvas backdrop of mountains. A few folding-chairs. And we find that we are

[*witnesses*]
still here—seated amid our usual greed and violence, watching the sketchily realistic playing of a scene in Stalin's home district—some proletarian pastoral in the

[*witnesses as actors*]
already there—seated amid the ruins of the village. Smoking, chatting, drinking. Two collectives in this circle —goatherds on the right, fruit-growers on the left—

1945 of a future that never
was.

A pause, and we watch the
debate. But we know what
ruthless power sustains an
affable Delegate from the
State Reconstruction Com-
mission. How real is "social-
ist realism"? Can we believe
in that agriculturalist with the
square face of Angelika
Hurwicz or whomever? A
game for children in a ring!

But rip-offs are still a way of
life in the Caucasus. Justice
is always ambiguous. What is
this leftist nostalgia for a
paradise unfound?

But wait: we're fools for a
story, if the Singer has the
shrewd eyes of Ernst Busch
or whomever—and if we can
play the players.

—had better find justice in
our world. How will the
voice of Brecht sound in the
shadow of tanks and bomb-
ers? Reserving judgment,

*who will judge their own
dispute. "Our beautiful dairy
farm: nothing but rubble." "I
set that fire, comrade." An
awkward pause, and we play
the relaxed debate between
those who want their old
home, though grass is sparse,
and those who need this valley for orchards and vine-
yards. Then the agriculturalist Kato bears witness to the
project for irrigation: a ten-
fold increase in fruit! "The
home of the Soviet people
shall also be the home of
reason." The issue is re-
solved: justice is on the left.
Nostalgia must yield to the
plan for greater production.
We embrace, prepare to
celebrate.*

*". . . we have arranged to put on
a play related to our problem.
Arkadi Cheidze, the singer, will
take part." He has asked almost
the whole collective of fruit-
growers to help him. And the
goatherds will witness the play.*

*"Comrades, your play had better be
good. . . ."*

*—it will cost us a valley. How
will the voice of the old poet
sound in the shadow of Soviet
tractors? But first, to share food,*

we break the circle for a moment. Now palace door and
cathedral door wheel into place, a city backdrop billows to
the floor like some Chinese watercolor scroll, the Singer and
his two musicians sit on the stage to our left, and his tenor

We Begin to Play Joining the Action
voice opens the first song: "In olden times, in bloody times. . . ."

[witnesses]

[witnesses as actors
as witnesses]

And we are already here.
Have the goatherds be-
come us? We have been
led from a factitious
realism into the
real theatricalism
of legend. Must
we learn that
to witness
is to
act?

And we are already here. Have we
become the goatherds' expanded
imagination? The style is leading us
into the action. And we begin to
witness the monstrous but ironically
providential world that is ours.
What we'll learn won't apply in
detail to the Prologue's world of
romantic rationalism. But humane
learning always applies to a new
situation—which is already here. Is
the play seducing us? If so, we're
learning our roles. As we enter circles of increasing moral complexity,
we'll be following a seductive course
in the art of playing. How else
could prudent spectators ever become mother, father, or judge?
How else could the valley bear
fruit?

Off-stage music—clarinets, trumpets, flute, drums—is now
accompanying the Singer: "One Easter Sunday morning. . . ."

[witnesses as actors
as witnesses]
And playing the witnesses, we
enter a world of extremes:
beggars' rags and the fixed
faces of those who deny their
humanity. In this political
farce, what life?

[witnesses as actors
as actors]
And playing the players, we
demonstrate 'going to church.'
Wearing masks from folk-tale
or dream, the Governor's
retinue pretend to adore the
noble child.

"The city lies silent. . . ."

But suddenly it's a more hu-
manely comic world—where
peasant faces and witty voices

Now it's a light interlude, an
anonymous flirtation. Our agriculturalist becomes the kitch-

mask an urgent passion. To witness and be witnessed, down by the willows, was already to enter the action. And now the Singer's voice becomes more ominous—

enmaid, our wounded soldier her admirer. *I joke as we always joke. I answer with a proper indignation. But we intend the circle of marriage.*

"Noon was a time for dying. . . ."

—and that political farce has become melodrama. We recognize an old story:

Now we play the fall of the great. *We Ironshirts do what we always do.*

"O blindness of the great! . . ."

—and taunt the grey-faced Governor. Now melodrama, farce, and humane comedy all converge. But when Grusha's rhythmic speech moves into song, her plain declaration of fidelity

So we play the condemned Governor, fleeing servants, doctors abandoning the child, and Grusha accepting the pig-headed soldier's shy proposal before he can make it: *when you return I'll be there.*

"I will be waiting for you under the green elm tree
I will be waiting for you under the bare elm tree
I will be waiting till the last has come home again"

expresses all we'd say if we knew how. She is our Singer and her own. And when the false mother abandons her child, Grusha finds a second commitment. Again to witness and be witnessed is already to have entered the action. And so our own witnessing now seems to merge with hers. The meaning? Intimacy

And even more. But now the two plots converge as we play the flight of the Governor's wife and the seduction of the kitchenmaid by the child: *He's looking at me. He's somebody.* Of course she puts him down. Frightened by the Governor's bloody head, she starts to leave. But at the Singer's words,

"As she stood there between door and archway, she heard
Or thought she heard a faint cry. . . ."

crosses a distance. We hear speech in silence.

she stands rooted. He speaks the voice of the child.

" 'Woman,' he said, 'help me.' . . ."

We are with Grusha as she is   and we silently mime her at-
with the child. Hearing, we   tempt to refuse—as the city
witness her reluctant discovery   burns, and night falls. and
that she has already   there is no one else.

"Terrible is the temptation to do good!"

joined the action. And now we   And when the seduction is
must engage the moral am-   complete, *I bend down and*
biguity of virtue: *pick up the child:*

"Like a thief she crept away."
A brief interlude now from the off-stage
instruments, palace-door and cathedral
door wheel out of sight, a mountain
backdrop unrolls,

WE PLAY THE RELUCTANT HEROISM OF FLIGHT
                and Singer and
    Musicians begin an antiphonal song:
        "When Grusha Vachnadze left the city
          On the Gruzinian military highway. . . ?"

    "How can she, so human, hope
    To escape the bloodhounds, the setters of snares?'

[*witnesses as actors*   [*witnesses as actors*
   as witnesses]   *as actors*]
Are we distancing ourselves   Now we sing with Grusha a
further from the action? Yes: wry song of the lucky hero,
time is speeding up; sets will   play the murderous business
wheel into view as needed. But   of selling milk to the hungry,
don't we participate more inti-   relish the tired lust of the Iron-
mately? Yes: we answer the   shirts, feel the child's increas-
Singer now through the Musi-   ing weight, know that she must
cians; and Grusha's own songs   give him away—and also play
now begin to express more than   the witnesses of this action.
a kitchenmaid's meanings.   For when the Singer
When the Singer asks,   asks,

    "Why so happy, woman returning homeward?"

our chorus of Musicians an-   our chorus of Musicians an-
swers for Grusha: swers for Grusha:

"Because with a smile, the helpless child has
Got himself new parents, I am happy."

And when he asks,   And when he asks,

"And why so sad?"

our chorus answers: our chorus answers:

"Because I am free and unburdened, I am sad. . . ."

As we could sing for her, can't   But when Grusha has saved the
she now sing for us?   child again, the song is hers:

"Since no one wants to take you, child
I shall have to take you."

And after crossing the bridge,   Before risking two lives on
she sings for us an ironic myth   the rotten bridge, *I sing again.*
of the good that is born from   And after crossing, *I sing "The*
apparent evil: *Song of the Child":*

"*The tiger's son will*
Feed the little foals his brothers
The child of the serpent
Bring milk to the mothers."
From our various removes, we now play
through her the role of the eponymous
Mother—Grusha of Gruzinia. Are we
ready for a wedding and a golden age
of peace? No: this convergence has
been too easy. Another interlude from
the off-stage instruments, a backdrop
of a mountain village unrolls,

We Play the Failing Heroism of Accommodation
                              the
          Singer describes Grusha's descent from
          the glacier, a peasant hut appears,

[*witnesses as actors*   [*witnesses as actors*
as witnesses]   *as actors*]
and we witness how she be-   and we play her entrance into
comes a more self-conscious   the house of the cowardly
player—yes, like us. She sings brother. *I wait through the*
the shrewd words that a be-   *winter; I sing by the loom a*
trothed once said to her lover: *lullaby to my child:*

" 'Dearest love, dearest love
If you must go off to war . . .
Keep in the middle of the war . . .
Those in the middle come home again.' "

Mustn't we find the center of peace through the center of war? Grusha must therefore enter the brother's plot. In the middle of our play, let's have an ironic celebration—wedding and funeral! A scene out of Breughel! But both tricksters must be tricked. And then the Singer must lead us beyond all such would-be clever evasions into the lyric	*Michael, we must be clever— we must join in the plot for a death-bed marriage with the draft-evading peasant. We play a prudent celebration—my wedding and his funeral. But when peace is declared, who has the worst of the bargain— the peasant married without a wife or Grusha married without Simon? So we play her life by the stream*

"As by the brook she sat washing the linen
She saw his face in the water. . . ."

heart of trouble. We must now witness the child's growth and Simon's return—to play the true father? Not yet. Once, the mutual understanding of Simon and Grusha could outrun their peasant speech. Not now. Through the Singer, we must sing what they thought but could not say. He:	*and the child's play—as he learns to play the false father in the Heads-Off game. And we play the meeting of Simon and Grusha on opposite banks of the stream. The laconic formulas of passion no longer serve. With the Singer, we mime what they thought but could not say. He:*

"To eat I had aspen buds, to drink I had maple broth,
I slept at night on stones, or in water."

And she:	*And she:*

"I had to tear myself to pieces for what was not mine
A stranger."

As they stand there, separated by misunderstanding, we are with them both. But how can our witnessing prevent catastrophe? How can it become present within the performed action?	*This stream is crossed only by our broken playing. Can such playing bring us all to the center? When the child is captured, Grusha must be judged by one who plays the player.*

"Who will the judge be? A good one? A bad one?
The city was in flames. On the seat of justice sat Azdak."
The Singer rises, steps into the wings.
An instrumental interlude recalls the
opening scenes of our legend, the City-
backdrop again billows to the floor,
a small hut appears,

WE PLAY LEARNING TO PLAY JUDGE
                                and the Singer,
played now by a second actor who has
been waiting in the wings, returns to
his seat and begins his song:
"Hear now the story of the judge
How he became judge, how he passed judgment, what
          manner of judge he is.
That Easter Sunday when the great uprising took place. . . ."

[witnesses as actors as witnesses]

And we are already here. Witnessing again the fall of the great—but our witnessing continues to transform itself into the playing it already is. He who was Singer now plays Azdak—and we enter the action with him.

[witnesses as actors as witnesses and actors]

And we are already here. Playing again the fall of the great—but, in accord with Brecht's own direction of the Berliner Ensemble, our first Singer now steps into the action that our second Singer narrates. Ernst Busch or whoever—dressed in rags and slightly drunk—is helping an old beggar into his hut. Now more fully inside and outside the action, we'll follow this subplot till it converges with the main plot. Through the Singer narrating Azdak, through the player who is lightly estranged from Azdak, through Azdak who is mordantly estranged from himself in each momentary role he plays, we'll act and witness this cowardly man of wry wit and radical sympathies, this clever trimmer and impersonator who is in the act of turning into a judge. And so the ironic consciousness which had been defied by the

Sit down and eat, here's a piece of cheese. . . . What were you running for. . . . Shits? Let's see your hand. . . . White. . . . A phoney . . . a landowner . . . don't deny it, I can tell by your guilty look!

Prologue, appeased by Grusha's seduction by goodness, and then invited to cooperate with the plotting in the northern mountains, now can locate and judge itself in this rascally role—a role which can also be seduced by good- *You're surprised, aren't you?* ness, and through which we *That I didn't hand you over.* can play a saturnalia of justice. *But I couldn't even hand a bed-* More detached from the action *bug over to that dumb-ox* than ever, participating more *policeman. . . .* fully than ever, we explore a slippery but sharable playing that no one can possess. In and through Azdak, intellectual skepticism and histrionic nihilism give themselves to the field of play—and discover the real.

We act and witness Azdak's saving and abandoning the disguised Grand Duke, and then—beneath the hanged judge in the court of justice—his self-denunciation to avoid punishment. With him we sing a song of injustice, *Our men are taken away, scattered to all four winds, so that the noble lords at home may feast and revel,* and with his dull pupil Shauva we sound the refrain, *Yes, yes, yes, yes, it's so.* With Azdak we act and witness his evasion when he finds that he'd mistaken his captors *Didn't I tell you I let him go?* and his playing of the condemned Grand Duke in order to judge for the Ironshirts the Fat Prince's candidate for judge. Isn't he learning all the roles? *Young man, earnestly advise not fall into clipped military delivery in public.* He plays with such satirical sympathy that, when the Ironshirts appoint him the new judge, we find ourselves shouting with them: *The judge was always a blackguard, so now let a blackguard be judge.* The whole play seems to have become ours—or have we become the play's? After pulling back for a scene-changing song with our new Singer and the chorus of Musicians, we enter the court to act and witness the simultaneous hearing of two cases (having had some practice in such splitting of attention), the acquitting of the negligent doctor, the fining of the invalid investor, and the bribing of the blackmailer. Another scene-changing song, and we enter from the highroad to convict the voluptuous daughter-in-law for raping the stableman. Considering not legality but motives, we live through our rascal-redeemer a delightful parable of strict justice plus graft. Another scene-changing song, and we enter a tavern to defend an old woman against the prosperous farmers—and to recite a litany to the Bereaved Mother Gruzinia. Are we now ready to help Grusha of Gruzinia? Through Singer and Musicians we sum up our saving disorder:

"So he bent the regulations to his own interpretations
And he took the law and stretched it on a rack."

Surely we've now answered the false Easter with which our legend
began, and have fulfilled the prophetic "Song of the Child?" No:
this saturnalia of an uncrucified rogue has been too easy. We have
brought no more than a temporary comic justice to our social
rascality. So when the Grand Duke and the Governor's Wife return, we must sing with Azdak the "Song of Chaos" in lament for
the passing of a good time, and Azdak must now panic *I'm afraid
of death* and agree to oblige the Governor's Wife *The child will be
brought back, your highness* by bringing to Grusha the usual justice
She will be beheaded, your highness. After all, what else can we
expect of ourselves?

By inviting us to participate in a joyous commitment to justice
that is inseparable from a cowardly evasion, our play has unfolded
the seamy texture of our moral world. That faced, can we now explore what it might mean to have the courage of our playful convictions? All exit. No interlude, no scene-change,
WE PLAY IN THE CENTER OF THE CIRCLE
                              but we know that Grusha must now fully
enter the world of our present playing—as we must fully enter
that in which she is played. Through the slippery Azdak, our most
questionable self-judging witness-actor, we'll be with her—as with
everyone, of whatever moral condition.

"Hear now the story of the lawsuit. . . ."

First the child: hold Grusha back while we lead him across the
stage. His moment will come. Then Grusha's unsettling but heartening discovery that one whom she thinks absent is truly present. *I
can't worry my head about him now if he doesn't understand.* But
Simon is already here: *I am ready to swear, I am the father of the
child.* Another witness has more fully entered the action, and the
moral ambiguity of virtue begins to assume an ironically theatrical
form: truth in lies, real presence in seeming absence. But with the
Ironshirts we shout: *Where's the Judge?*—for we need him to sustain
the focus of our detached yet participatory playing. Has he given
us the slip? Then Grusha's second discovery that one whom she
thinks absent—the Ironshirt she had hit over the head—is present.
Do you know her? Terrifying—but heartening. Again the answer
is a lying truth: *No.* Does a real presence lurk within that moral
absence?

When the Governor's Wife and her lawyers take the stage, everything's set to move. But what? Ironshirts and Farmers are dragging in Azdak, who *has* been running away—*Take off his robe before you string him up!* Must the story of the judge begin all over again? As we act and witness the Ironshirts' kicking Azdak this way and that, their throwing him back and forth, his face increasingly bloodied, it's the roughest scene in the play—the hardest to distance ourselves from, the hardest to take. And yet in the midst of this frenzy some part of us is clapping hands hysterically along with the Governor's Wife. A fake violence? We know better than that—and so does Azdak. *Greetings, dogs! . . . Licking the old boot again? Back at each other's throats, dogs?* And when the Rider brings a dispatch that appoints Azdak judge—yes, once more the old *deus ex machina* trick—another truth emerges from these compounded theatrical lies. Who can play the true judge? Only the scapegoat who has been mocked, tortured, and sentenced to death. Between that sentence and a final disappearance, during the brief reprieve made possible by a lucky convergence of events and a seduction by goodness, a true presence may judge our case through a role now intensely aware of its own potential absence—its chronic evasion of responsibility and its essential transience. Azdak has fainted. Coming to life again, dressed again in the judge's robe, he sways precariously as he walks toward the Ironshirts—and with him we know that whoever bears witness to truth can make only a fleeting appearance on a stage of lies.

Now let each role declare its shared fragment of our contradictory condition. Through the lawyers, the Governor's Wife, and Azdak: our faked emotions and chronic venality. *The court looks upon your mention of the estates as proof that we're all human.* Through Azdak and Simon: our willingness to lie in order to play our true roles. *I'm the father, your worship.* Through Grusha and Azdak: our willingness to let truth speak through silence or spontaneous irrelevance. *Did the child come from whoring?* No answer. *Did he have refined features? He showed a nose in his face.* Yes— a significant answer. *There's a story they tell about me; . . . once before pronouncing a verdict I went out and sniffed at a rosebush.* But now, after the capping of proverbs and the trading of insults, let Azdak's mordantly playful absence as true judge unleash Grusha's indignant judgment of all judges: *I'll tell you one thing: for a job like yours they should only pick rapists and usurers, to punish them by making them sit in judgment over their fellow men, which is worse than hanging on the gallows.* She bears witness to justice itself. And now—after a moment of contrapuntal attention to the old

back-to-back couple who, mutually dependent in their contrariness,
think they want a divorce but are really a playful image of our dialectic—we're ready to let Grusha be tested. Isn't *she* being unjust to
the child? *Don't you want him to be rich?* Silence. *Hear now*, announces the Singer, *what the angry woman thought but did not say*
—and for the last time, song articulates a silent speech:

"If he walked in golden shoes
Cold his heart would be and stony. . . ."

But our lyric witnessing has now fully entered the action: attentive
to Grusha's silence, the Azdak who is being played by one who
was Singer now hears this song. It's as easy as sniffing a rosebush.
Woman, I think I understand you. When we no longer construe
acting and witnessing to be merely external relations among self-
closed entities, when we allow the field of play to become actual
among us, we can all be brought into the center. Let Shauva now
bring in the child. And let the child—Michael or the child who
plays him, who can tell the difference?—engage Azdak, Grusha,
and us who play them in a moment of smiling reciprocity. Let
that moment speak its meaning against all the possessive and an-
tagonistic words of the Governor's Wife. The delighted child who
sits on Azdak's knee as he directs Shauva to draw a circle is almost an image of what we must again become. *Put the child in the
circle.* Of course. And who would want to drag him out—or, worse,
use him as rope for tug of war? Nevertheless: *Pull!* No: Grusha's
spontaneous gesture is at one with our own resistance: *I didn't hold
on to him.* Her non-action, a true action, bears witness for her.
All right, I'll repeat the test to make sure. Azdak now smilingly
tyrannical, Grusha reduced to despair: surely what belongs to us,
what we care for, is just what we can't hold on to? *I can't.* At once,
as Azdak rises from the judge's chair and begins to disrobe, we act
and witness the true judge's simultaneous emergence from the mask
of absence and abandonment of the judicial role. Hearing the verdict, we share Grusha's discovery of yet another unexpected presence. And now let one last whimsically right mistake—the divorce
of the wrong couple—enable all our roles to come together in the
final dance, our miming of the green or golden world of order which
is always the goal of our festive play. Into that dance Azdak himself
must now disappear.

As our Singer moralizes on this "brief Golden Age when there
was almost justice," we share the closing words as witnesses and

actors who have been led step by step into a circle of reciprocity
and so understand how our play enacts a complex critique of the
Prologue's utopian reason.

"And the valley to those who water it, that it may bear fruit."
We understand (as Brecht himself granted) that the play is no "parable" told "in order to clear up the argument about who owns the valley." The story, he said, "of itself proves nothing but merely displays
a particular kind of wisdom." But we also understand that the play
is more than a story, and that the pattern of our shared acting and
witnessing hasn't been narrowly economic or political in its wisdom. It has transcended both the sardonic doubt that the later
Brecht always tried to purge from his thought and the Marxist
dogma that he could let stand as a strategic half-truth. Certainly we
are now neither editorializing peasants nor intellectual skeptics.
What has been our dramatic experience? The Prologue aroused our
desire to see justice done, to enter the action, to play in truth the
golden age. But as we continued, our emergent objective became
ever more clearly "to bear witness." To what? To our chronic greed,
violence, and corruption. And to our vulnerability, when meeting
the human, to the terrible temptation and necessity of goodness.
Our experience of a strangely spontaneous ability to follow the leading of that temptation has here been inseparable from the self-
opening and self-abandoning movements that have shaped this field
of playful convergence. Who then are the waterers? Who are we?
Witnesses who have become actors, actors who have become witnesses, transient roles in a field of creative responsibility that can
finally be possessed by no one.

We may water the valley, raise the child, judge the case, play
the role—but there is finally no question of holding onto anything.
"When your work is done," says the Tao-te-Ching, "disappear." The
self-exiled poet and ostensible Marxist who wrote our script (and
who seems often to have silenced his mind concerning the pro-
founder meanings of his dramatic structures) had an oddly appropriate affection for that supra-political but not unpolitical set
of aphorisms. That's why we must now—like Azdak, and like the
old man in Brecht's "Legendary Origin of the Book Tao-te-Ching
during Lao-Tse's Journey into Exile"—gladly look back at the
valley of our playing and forget it. In the end we must do without
Azdak or any player as we must do without ourselves. Only in
another spontaneously fruitful playing may we find, for a moment,
our true roles in the circle.

Celebrating

here and now: finding in these particulars the eternal design. For us, not likely. This barren church. These uncomfortable seats. Screens hiding the altar. But we wait, skeptics and nominal believers, theater-goers lured by the facile attraction of murder in a cathedral. Voices enter behind.

Here let us stand, close by the cathedral. Here let us wait.

Women hurrying, pausing. Making their way down the aisles. Confused little groups in autumnal browns, wintry black. Poor worshippers of twelfth-century Canterbury? No. Not quite worshippers. Nor merely then and there. Restless bodies among us. Anxious voices echoing our own expectancy, uncertainty, resistance. But afraid, as we are not?

Some presage of an act
Which our eyes are compelled to witness, has forced our feet
Towards the cathedral. We are forced to bear witness.

And we? Compelled toward an almost liturgical participation in the reluctant witnessing of these women? They huddle there, played by, or playing, the Chorus: a presage of what act?

The New Year waits, breathes, waits, whispers in darkness.

No act, surely, that is so external as Becket's murder. Nothing merely in history.

And who shall
Stretch out his hand to the fire, and deny his master?

In this festival re-membering at the turn of the year, the past is future. And the locus of our playing? Some tacit but freshly agitated field among us. Whispering. Made audible, visible, in these choral figures. But if so, what of Becket?

Seven years since the Archbishop left us . . .

Eight hundred years since Becket was murdered. Two thousand years since . . .

But it would not be well if he should return.

Who shall stretch out his hand? To what end do we remember him now? Suddenly emerging from the Chorus, a single voice.

Destiny waits in the hand of God, shaping the still unshapen.
I have seen these things in a shaft of sunlight.

And I? Can I see in this playing what "we perceive in our own lives only at rare moments of inattention and detachment drowsing in the sunlight"? The pattern? The end, for Eliot, toward which poetic drama moves? But how grasp what is given to the nongrasping?

Shall the Son of Man be born again in the litter of scorn?
For us, the poor, there is no action,
But only to wait and to witness.

For us, must waiting and witnessing somehow become the action?

From behind the screens, three Priests in Benedictine habit. Or those who play at Priests. Speaking with a slightly comic Messenger, a self-conscious prognosticator, who has watched Becket's triumphal entrance into Canterbury. Professional witnesses. No less anonymous than the Chorus. No less anxious.

I fear for the Archbishop, I fear for the Church . . .

Earnest youth, alert to pride of prosperity, adversity, virtue. Therefore afraid.

The Archbishop shall be at our head, dispelling dismay
and doubt . . .

Effusive middle age, weaving a dream of security. Also afraid.

For good or ill, let the wheel turn . . .

Laconic age, seeing the emptiness of all temporal power. Unafraid? Or hiding fear in a lofty indifference? Echoing the Preacher's words—

And all the daughters of music shall be brought low.

—which continue to echo silently among us: "they shall be afraid of that which is high, and fears shall be in the way." Yes. As if by contagion, a tremor now running through the Chorus.

Forcing confession of their private terrors, their particular shadows. Ours, too? And more—

> *a fear not of one but of many,*
> *A fear like birth and death, when we see birth and death alone*
> *In a void apart. We*
> *Are afraid in a fear which we cannot know, which we cannot*
> *face, which none understands . . .*

And we? But there's no need to approach that shattering emptiness or anonymity. Better to distance this hysteria.

> *What a way to talk at such a juncture!*

And so we babble with the Second Priest against their babbling— in our fear of fear?

Another figure now. Travelling cloak over his habit. Still, commanding. A hand raised in benediction.

> *Peace. And let them be . . .*

At last: no anxious anonymity but a named individual, Becket himself—who knows how to act.

> *They know and do not know, what it is to act or suffer.*
> *They know and do not know, that action is suffering*
> *And suffering is action. Neither does the agent suffer*
> *Nor the patient act. But both are fixed*
> *In an eternal action, an eternal patience*
> *To which all must consent that it may be willed*
> *And which all must suffer that they may will it . . .*

The design glimpsed in a shaft of sunlight? No: only a form of words. But words that would seem to require—what? Not only Becket's entrance into an anonymity beyond the fear of death and birth, but ours? Suppose it possible. Suppose this named individual has emerged within our field of play only so that he may discard a delusory power of self-determination. Suppose our sharing, somehow, in that gesture. Pride and fear dissolved, no "I" presuming to act or suffer. How could our playing disclose such a transpersonal opening to . . .

End will be simple, sudden, God-given.
Meanwhile the substance of our first act
Will be shadows, and the strife with shadows.

Surely not by letting this *persona* cast himself now as protagonist, actor, and director of a play-within-our-play? Note
the cool arrogance in this self-reflexive posing. Note how his
glance takes us in as he seats himself now before us.

All things prepare the event. Watch.

Becket—or he who plays him?—speaking now not only to
Priests and Chorus but also to us in the nave. Our fields of play
merging with his, as we wait together.

You see, my Lord, I do not wait upon ceremony . . .

From the corner of the platform, what shadow darting forward
with jingling speech? Some Fellowship for this Everyman? Gay
courtier's costume, flaunting a plume. But in this context no
merely allegorical figure: more sharply particularized than
Chorus or Priests. A historical presence, remembered. As solid
for Becket as Becket is for us.

Voices under sleep, waking a dead world,
So that the mind may not be whole in the present.

And yet dismissed as impossible, undesirable. At once from
another corner:

Your Lordship has forgotten me, perhaps.

A more solidly historical presence. Met at Clarendon, at North-
ampton, at Montmirail. Remembered now, a suave embodiment
of diplomatic maturity. A potential colleague.

Shall he who held the solid substance
Wander waking with deceitful shadows?
Power is present.

No: the temptation of a deceitful shadow that must be dismissed.

. . . shall I, who keep the keys
Of heaven and hell, supreme alone in England,

Who bind and loose, with power from the Pope,
Descend to desire a punier power?

But dismissed by whom? By a yet subtler shadow who doesn't
know himself to be such? With what aplomb now dismissing in
advance the yet more grotesquely solid visitor who pops up in
the far corner.

No purpose brings surprise.

Portly, bluff, circuitous: a lord from the country. Proposing a
happy coalition of intelligent interests. Fatuous embodiment of
another thought: to make, then break,

The desperate exercise of failing power.

Again no real temptation. What does tempt this subtle shadow
of power?

. . . if I break, I must break myself alone.

But can the breaker break himself? Can the will annihilate the
will? Can Becket dismiss himself?

Well done, Thomas, your will is hard to bend.

A voice from behind him. Or behind us. Slightly echoing through
the nave. Almost, in tone and cadence, the voice of Thomas.
A presence indistinct in the shadows—and yet more firmly
among us than any previous visitor.

Who are you?

Becket facing us, eyes wide. And the echo:

As you do not know me, I do not need a name.
And, as you know me, that is why I came.

A strange duel now. Within Thomas. Among us. As the arrogantly reflexive *persona* in our field of play meets himself in the
mirror. And so unfolds the desire for spiritual power, the fear
of transience, which he *is*. No more than the other three is this
fourth visitor a tempter. Rather, a satanic good angel: clarifying
that temptation which has already been proposed and accepted
by a Thomas who thinks himself actor and sufferer.

Seek the way of martyrdom, make yourself the lowest
On earth . . .

But to what end, in this shared solitude, can our powerful and self-deceptive shadow meet his own shadow? What can he now *do*?

> *Is there no way, in my soul's sickness,*
> *Does not lead to damnation in pride?*

It's the ego's double-bind, the doubt-block of our theater, the trap of every inauthentic self which dreams of abolishing itself.

> *Can I neither act nor suffer*
> *Without perdition?*

And the echo.

> *You know and do not know, what it is to act or suffer.*
> *You know and do not know . . .*

A riddle for Thomas. A *koan* posed by the subliminal spiritual director whom he has arrogantly challenged. A form of words that no individual, as such, can rightly understand. To which no *persona* claiming to be an entity can adequately respond. Words requiring our entrance into an anonymity beyond the fear of death and birth.

That the pattern may subsist, that the wheel may turn and still
Be forever still.

And now to be manifest in our playing? Thomas doesn't move. Silence. Restless movements now begin among the women of the Chorus.

> *Thick and heavy the sky. And the earth presses up against*
> > *our feet.*

From the four visitors a self-mocking ditty.

> *All things become less real, man passes*
> *From unreality to unreality.*

A cry of fear from the Priests.

O Thomas my Lord do not fight the intractable tide . . .

The outer reaches of our field in feverish response to this moment of self-blockage. And joining now in a threefold antiphonal chant—

Is it the owl that calls, or a signal between the trees?

Voices among us, within us, crying our apprehension of death. Our unavoidable commitment to death. The death that constitutes this very self which tries to flee or vanquish death. Voices now resolving into an ode of despair that rises to hysterical pitch.

Puss-purr of leopard, footfall of padding bear,
Palm-pat of nodding ape, square hyaena waiting
For laughter, laughter, laughter.

The Lords of Hell *are* here. Whatever our intellectual or spiritual pretensions, these women now cry out for *us*—in their necessary confusion.

. . . save us, save us, save yourself that we may be saved;
Destroy yourself and we are destroyed.

As if Thomas, or even the tempted savior whose imperfect figure he may be, could ever save himself—except by losing himself. As if anyone could be saved through his act except by participating in that self-losing. Isn't this call from the Chorus to Thomas really a signal between the trees, a signal from and to ourselves? No, not our*selves*. A signal from and to the one agent, the one patient, through the transient multiplicity of our field of play. Absurd to assume that Thomas now hears the Chorus as a man who thinks himself to be a subject in a field of objects might hear a crowd of women. Absurd to say that Eliot here has scanted the playwright's duty to render his protagonist's moment of decision. This moment doesn't belong to Thomas. We belong to this moment. In the performed action, no individual self now makes a temporal decision to act: this decision, as Thomas will later say, is taken "out of time." And within the action of performance, aren't we aware that this named *persona*, though more sharply individualized than Priests and Chorus, is a mask for us—a mask for our mask-wearing? So now: behind the mask, behind the voices and the silence, here among us in our field of co-presence—an eternal action, an eternal patience. Quick now, here, now, always—in the eternal moment for which *Four Quartets* sought ampler verbal equivalents. In this moment, Thomas is lost. Freed, for the moment, from the pretense of being someone.

Now is my way clear, now is the meaning plain . . .

And, after the experience of this moment, who speaks? A *persona* newly aware that he is such. In effect, a new *persona*? Speaking to us, and for us, as if *raisonneur* of this playing which we are—with the distortions of language that such a role requires.

The last temptation is the greatest treason.
To do the right deed for the wrong reason.

As if it could ever be merely a choice of reasons. Does the moment of opening seem past? Have we missed it? If so,

I know
What yet remains to show you of my history
Will seem to most of you at best futility,
Senseless self-slaughter of a lunatic. . . .

Or do we glimpse it even now? Is Thomas now our imperfect mask for what may be born in the moment of the self's attentive death? If so,

I shall no longer act or suffer, to the sword's end.

Not I, but who? Becoming no one, beginning to live. For this *persona*, waiting and witnessing must now be the action. And for us? Or must we continue to witness in the mirror of our playing our own fear of bearing witness?

Darkness for a while. Now lights slowly up. The Chorus has joined us in the front rows. Or, compelled yet further, have we joined them? Thomas—he who has glimpsed the emptiness of the *persona* he seems to be—enters, mounts the pulpit.

Dear children of God, my sermon this Christmas morning
will be a very short one.

A festival remembering within our festival remembering—or including it? An expounding of the masses of Christmas Day: on this anniversary of birth-into-death, the ritual anamnesis of death-into-birth. For him who plays Thomas, as for us who play ourselves, that ritual anamnesis is now becoming a present action. Thomas tells us as much in the Christian language that we now seem precariously to share—for the design of this play is increasingly focusing the spectrum of our acting-and-witnessing as an analogue to the experience of martyrdom.

But if so, how can our glimpse of the contradictory emptiness of "self" now inform the gestural language of our continued playing? Can such a moment of "death"—when something not ourselves may be born again in the litter of our lives—shape an action that is extended through time? Must the *persona* who now seems primarily to focus our field of play cease utterly to be a performer? And must the actor somehow let a non-histrionic protagonist become present through him? If it's true that powerful acting is always the miming of "acting"—the playing for us of a character's conscious or unconscious mask-wearing—surely *Murder in the Cathedral* will now sacrifice its strongest dramatic possibilities and become a mere charade or rite?

But consider: even such a charade or rite must remain in some sense histrionic. In this very sermon, Thomas remains the homiletic artist, the orator, the performer. He is presenting to his congregation a deliberately constructed mask. And as the members of this congregation who are closest to the interiority of his action, we know that behind the mask of pastoral care he now understands "himself" also to be a mask—a self-emptying *persona* through which a design may be realized. Doesn't Thomas in fact now understand "himself" much as the actor who plays him must understand "Thomas"—and also "*himself*"? For both, the scenario is given. The performance must go on. But no authentic performance can now result from a self-aggrandizing imposition of will. Both "Thomas" and "the actor" must remain aware that they are enabled to participate

in a design not of their own making—and that they are hence-
forth masks within a celebratory event. For both, the performance must therefore be to an unusual degree an alert miming
that is held open to the possibility of transfiguration by a momentary rightness. Isn't that why Robert Speaight, in working
toward the first performance at Canterbury in 1935, found that
the true actor's initiatives must be "the initiatives of grace"?

Not that playing the martyr on stage is no different from
playing a martyr to the death. Only our vanity could collapse
the analogy. And won't the presence of those other masks for
our various condition—Chorus, Priests, and Knights—continue
to remind us of our distance from Thomas? Nevertheless, both
kinds of action would be worse than meaningless if not constituted through a sequence of those little deaths that may allow a fresh response to what speaks in the present. Even on
December 29, the day of his death, Thomas must still say, "I
have therefore only to make perfect my will." What will? Not
that egocentric will which has long been so hard to bend, but a
disciplined attention to the moment. For when "I" give myself
to what the Third Priest will call the "critical moment / That
is always now, and here," action and patience may then be
given. In this moment the persona may no longer act from a
personal consciousness—that self-contradictory knot of energy
which seeks to grasp its own history and project it into the
future—but may open upon a witnessing consciousness of lucidity and spontaneity. For the actor—but only after patient
study of the script and detailed interpretation of the role in collaboration with the ensemble of players—such disciplined attention must mean an alert detachment within each sentence,
gesture, or psychic movement: a detachment that may enable an
improvisatory freshness, the genuineness of moment-by-moment
discovery. For both Thomas and the actor, any deliberate action (their "waiting" and "witnessing") will doubtless be primarily negative—not *that* false move, not *that* habitual reaction,
not *that* chronically self-deceptive gesture, tone, or thought—a
series of instantaneous dismissals that may allow the emergence
of the authentic response to the given field of play. For both,
as for the poet of *Little Gidding*, every sentence must therefore

be an epitaph, every word and every gesture a step to the block. Only so can they see their way clear, find the meaning plain. Only for such a witness may all manner of things be well—and "all things / Proceed to a joyful consummation." Even at that, no joy becomes in this play a final possession: Thomas' last action will be to initiate a movement toward confession, and the Chorus' last action will be to complete that movement. In such ways the performed action will unfold in accord with its theological assumptions a bold image of the re-creative movement that makes possible our action of performance.

What follows in Part II for him who plays Thomas, as for him who plays the actor who plays Thomas, must therefore be a difficult charade that requires devoted attention—a rite that may be the occasion of graceful action. "Even now, in sordid particulars / The eternal design may appear." And for us who witness and so implicitly act Thomas, Chorus, Priests, and Knights, Part II of this play must also be such a charade or rite. We may know the scenario: the arrival of the Knights in a moment foreseen but unexpected; the ode in fear of the death-bringers among and within us; the consoling of the Chorus and the hurrying of Thomas to the cathedral; the ode in fear of our hellish emptiness, accompanied by the distant singing of the *Dies Irae*; the decision of Thomas—taken "out of time"—to open the cathedral door; the murder, taking place during the ode in confession and purgation of our foulness; the Knights' sudden stepping forward into *our* moment, the moment of this action of performance, to unfold for us (as the fourth visitor has done for Thomas) our complicity in the murder—by naming its import for a modern consciousness that has learned nothing from our shared playing; the Priests' variously partial responses to the martyrdom; and the final ode in confession and celebration, accompanied by the distant singing of the *Te Deum*, which completes the dramatic figure through which "the darkness declares the glory of light." But these foreseen steps in themselves guarantee neither for Thomas nor for us the meaning of what will happen. This script, as a script, *proves* nothing at all about Thomas' final spiritual state. It supports with finality neither the Fourth Knight's verdict of "Suicide while of Unsound Mind" nor the Third Priest's gratitude for "another Saint in Canterbury," and it gives no unambiguous endorsement to the Chorus' apparent recognition of shared responsibility for "the blood of the martyrs and the agony of the saints": "Blessed Thomas, pray for us." The script simply lacks the requisite specificity for such proof, support, or endorsement. That doesn't mean, however, that *Murder in the Cathedral* as a play is neutral or unresolved. It unfolds the Yes of playing by leading us through and beyond the empty self-negation of ego-life. But its mode is deliberately and appropriately that of an invitation that can be refused.

If actors and witnesses continue to attend to the transpersonal moment—here, now, always—the masks of the closing charade or rite may acquire an authenticity that will be evident in Thomas' tone and bearing and in the increasing clarity of our own participation in the dramatic design. This design, not grasped by the possessive intellect but glimpsed in moments of shared opening, will intimate our condition as no collection of individuals but a being-in-community who, despite chronic fear, can bear witness to an eternal ground. We will find ourselves uniting finally by intention not with the body that is here shown to die but with the present life onto which it opens. And we will find that the Chorus, in its final recognition of an infinite creative plenitude to which our courage of surrender is usually most inadequate, speaks eloquently for our condition.

But it does not follow that we will assent to the defenses of ecclesiastical power that are sometimes offered by Thomas as well as the Priests. Just as the acting-and-witnessing of *The Caucasian Chalk Circle* calls into question the seeming commitment of its Prologue to political revolution of a statist variety, so that of *Murder in the Cathedral* calls into question its own seeming commitment to an authoritarian political reaction. For the eternal design can be no more than contradictorily manifest in those ego-projections, those structures not of co-presence but of defensive absence, which are the agencies of temporal power. On that score, the Knights are correct enough. And if we reject the play's invitation to attend to the critical moment, we will remain within their world of pragmatic political power, of

common-sense psychology, and of linear time—and may very
well find them irritating caricatures of ourselves, distorting mirrors offered by a reactionary play that seems only to want to
trap us.

Either way, we are already committed to a continuing participation. In this barren church, on these uncomfortable seats,
as we hear Thomas' sermon now draw to its conclusion, we
know that the performance must go on: a miming that may mirror our continuing fear of the one action, the one patience—
or may be transfigured. For us as for the *dramatis personae*,
Part II of *Murder* is a scenario that risks opening itself—that
invites us to risk opening ourselves—to a meaning both in and
out of time, which may be discovered at every foreseen but unexpected moment: the ending of "I," the beginning of divine
play.

*I would have you keep in your hearts these words that I
say, and think of them at another time.*

＊＊＊＊＊＊＊＊＊＊＊

Waking

*to light. In a dark time? Yes, and on this stage. Through a
playing that must be both* theatrum mentis *and* theatrum mundi:
*a chiaroscuro image of the solitary consciousness and of the
histrionic world we share.*

                    *Here the imprisoned Sigismund will
be given a sleeping potion by his ambitious guard and mentor,
will be brought to the king, will rebel on finding that king no
true father, will be recaptured and sentenced to death, and will
be snatched from the scaffold to be made a puppet ruler. After
a further* coup d'état *and the death of that mentor beyond
whose politics he has ripened, he will turn to the window to
speak with the naked rabble who believe him the Lamb of God
—and will be shot by the new dictator's hired snipers. An image
of the soul's entrance into what Hofmannsthal called "our piti-
less modern reality"? Not that alone. The Tower resists translation into any one-dimensional statement. Hofmannsthal has
here stripped Calderón's* Life is a Dream *of its romantic com-*

plications, has re-imagined its protagonist with the aid of the homologous myth in Jacob Wassermann's Caspar Hauser, *and has projected the entire play against the implicit background of post–1914 Europe. The* Christian-Platonic *hieroglyphs that set forth to seventeenth-century spectators the dream of life— from the soul's original sin to its repentance and redemption— have become history-laden and problematic symbols for our modern consciousness. Theatrical allegory has become an apocalyptic realism in which we are invited to participate. "Now," wrote Martin Buber to Hofmannsthal on reading the 1925 version of this play, "one may again believe in the existence of tragedy in our time." And in the "stage version" of 1927, which yet more fully justifies Buber's tribute, perhaps we may find the common ground of our fragmented theater. For despite its currently unfashionable idiom, its operatic panache, and its signs of a theatrical dilemma that has been incompletely surmounted,* The Tower *focuses a remarkably full spectrum of action.*

More explicitly than in Rosmersholm, *the enclosed stage will here render the prison-house, cave, or grave that every ego constructs as its temporal world. (The "walls of the world," as Jacob Wassermann exclaimed to his* Caspar Hauser, *'are to press in upon you until they again become a prison.") Here we will mime our chronic and suicidal efforts to objectify appearances, to control history, to turn even the transcendent subject of all appearances into a consciously possessed object. But we must not leap into Ibsen's icy void. ("There is a doctrine whispered in secret," said Socrates in the* Phaedo, *"that man is a prisoner who has no right to open the door and run away; this is a great mystery which I do not quite understand.") We will find here, as in* The Ghost Sonata, *that the prison-house is a purgatorial furnace within which we share a dream-work that moves toward waking. Toward another vision of "The Isle of the Dead"? No: we must wake here to a present light in the darkness, a Sun no less immanent than transcendent, which acts and suffers in our play. ("Colors," said Goethe in the foreword to his* Theory of Colors, *"are the acts and sufferings of light." "Human beings," said Hofmannsthal in a parallel note for* Andreas, *"are the sufferings and acts of the spirit.") In this opera without music we must attend to words and gestures that point, as in* Three Sisters, Heartbreak House, *and* Break of Noon, *toward harmonies audible only in the breaking of all that "I" have presumed to own. ("All is vain," the ripened Sigismund will say, "except the conversation between spirit and spirit.") No less than in* Henry IV, The Balcony, *and* Endgame, *we must understand that the empirical self with its itch to grasp everything in this house of illusions is a tyrannizing mask or metaphor that can only get lost —one way or another. On this quasi-historical stage we must therefore let that self go, as in* The Caucasian Chalk Circle *and* Murder in the Cathedral, *by entering a celebration that may disclose true action to be a difficult non-action and playing the players to mean bearing witness. ("We will live together in the open," Sigismund will say to the unadorned and unaccommodated people.) And so, in an annihilating moment that is always now, we will step with our protagonist to the dawn-struck window of this imagined castle or prison-house—to speak with the new friends who call. ("For here is reality," as the masked Spirit says in Hofmannsthal's Prologue to* Antigone, *"and everything else / is similitude and a playing in a mirror.") But we will also, of course, play the murderers and the incompletely comprehending witnesses. . . .*

                    Director: But how can we play *The Tower* today? As a Reinhardt spectacle, fifty years too late? A nostalgic Salzburg Festival? Or an intriguing confrontation in the manner of Peter Brook—with just a *soupçon* of Artaud? Waxworks or the latest thing—isn't that how we always distance a threatening immediacy? "And if there is still one hellish, truly accursed thing in our time," Artaud said, "it is our dallying with forms, instead of being like victims burnt at the stake, signaling through the flames." Hofmannsthal had used similar words. In his imaginary conversation "On Characters in Novels and Plays," he let Balzac (who had spoken of Goethe's profound "conversations" with those colors "which he called the sufferings and acts of light") conclude with this bold gesture: "To read destinies where they are written—that is everything. To have the power to see them all as they consume them-

selves, these living torches. To see them all at once bound to
the trees of the enormous garden which is illuminated by their
blaze alone. . . ." Yes: self-consuming torches—the characters,
the authors, us.

And do we dare to consume ourselves in play-
ing what Hofmannsthal called the "individual and his epoch
seen as a myth?" Within that myth, as individual centers in a
post-Kantian world of appearance, trapped in Plato's cave with
no evident exit to the real, suffering a history that seems the
interaction of egocentric powers, can we find the meaning of
Sigismund's journey from the den of pre-existence through the
dream-dilemmas of tragic awareness and on to a resolution
beyond tragedy? Certainly that is no journey to defeat, though
most critics seem to have thought so. Again and again they've told
us that Hofmannsthal, in revising *The Tower* to eliminate the
redemptive myth of the Children's King and his army of orphans,
finally admitted the blackness of our situation. Alfred Schwarz
has praised him for "an unflinching, historic testimony and a
moving personal confession that the gathering night cannot be
shut out." Egon Schwartz has said that Hofmannsthal here "de-
nied himself the step through the wall" into a saving dimension.
Even Hofmannsthal's friend Carl Burckhardt thought it "hard
for him to extinguish that light of hope which ennobles all
tragedy, and to rest with a completely dark conclusion." Half-
truths—spoken by those who have simply not seen why Sigismund, for *us*, must point to "joyful signs" that he can't explain.
And why he must say at the end of this version for the stage:
"I feel far too well to hope." *That* light is what our playing
must make clear.

Not that it will be easy. This play asks us to
take the next step beyond Pirandello's *Henry IV* : to find the
action of the nameless man or prince who does *not* imprison
himself. We must move beyond our willed masks of individu-
ality and also beyond our pessimistic theater of masks. The Beggar in Hofmannsthal's *Salzburg Great Theatre of the World*
already knows what the man who plays Henry IV refuses to
learn: "Freedom is always near, but if you force your way to
it, then at once it is far." That Beggar knows too that such free-

dom is founded on an abyss. In *The Tower* we must descend—
as Hofmannsthal put it to Hermann Bahr in 1904, early in his
long task of reworking *La Vida es sueño*—"into the deepest
depths of the doubtful cave-kingdom 'I' " and there find "the
no-longer-I or the world." Not an external world in opposition
to that doubtful I, but the real world that is prior to such a
dreamed split.

We must discover that in ourselves we can do
nothing. Nothing but bear witness to either darkness or light—
for we are self-consuming moments in a conversation that begins for each only with acceptance of a present death. Isn't that
why Sigismund must move from the condition of feral and yet
noble man (a Caspar Hauser in his prison) through swift and
traumatic metamorphoses, each a death of what he has been, to
the condition of unaccommodated Man (a transpersonal ripeness beyond Lear)? And why Hofmannsthal could call him "a
burning-glass of our time"? Finally no *single* soul or psyche,
Sigismund brings into focus the realm that Martin Buber located not "within" any "me" but "between us." As Maurice
Friedman has shown—though he too accepts the usual view of
this play as testimony to the gathering night—Buber himself no
doubt contributed, by criticizing the fantasy of messianic victory in the first version of Act 5, to the revision that produced
this utterly realistic testimony to the meaning of dialogue in an
otherwise empty world. All is vain except the conversation
between spirit and spirit. And such conversation, as Buber and
Hofmannsthal knew, bears witness to the light that is its source,
medium, and end.

Exactly because Sigismund is a self-unmask-
ing mask that focuses the light in which we participate, he is
what Hofmannsthal—echoing Nietzsche with a characteristic
shift in meaning—once said a tragic hero must be: "the mask
of the god, the character who suffers for the others." The
actor who plays Sigismund must therefore play for us all. But
so must the other actors. As we present the spectrum of our
acting and suffering, from Sigismund's vulnerable transparency
to Olivier's fiery opacity, each actor must represent the whole
company—and all those in the theater. For the participation in

the performed action that is the goal of *The Caucasian Chalk Circle* and the unfolding assumption of *Murder in the Cathedral* must here become the clear ground of our play. Not that any such thing need be expounded on stage. "Situations are symbolic," said Hofmannsthal in *The Book of Friends*; "it is the weakness of modern men that they treat them analytically and so dissolve the magic."

How to keep that magic? First of all, by a firm departure from all so-called realism or naturalism. "Naturalism distorts Nature," as Hofmannsthal said, "because in imitating surfaces it loses sight of the inner connections, Nature's true mystery." In shaping our style, *The Tower*'s Shakespearean and baroque strategies will help us: an ambiguity of time and place (seventeenth-century Poland or Spain? eighteenth-century Germany? our own Weltbürgerlich Festival?), a clear social stratification (with various levels of diction and playing style), and a rich theatricality suspended between popular entertainment and a subtle disclosure of our condition. Think, for instance, of the vernacular roles: Olivier, that man of military destiny; Anton, the wryly faithful servant; the soldiers and peasants; the apocalyptic rabble. Each, while remaining close to his type, must find some contemporary accent of grossness or wit. Murderers, naive prophets, and casual witnesses will then press toward the edges of our field of play, engaging the audience and drawing them in. But Sigismund's mentor, Julian, can have only an implicit modernity. Perhaps the actor might study the deft professionalism and raging ambition of some secular equivalent of that Jesuit king-maker. And Basilius must seem even less modern. Yet don't we understand all too well his Byzantine theatricality—and the fear of impotence that motivates it? Genet might find the part very suggestive. Perhaps the actor can move toward just such a feverishly lyrical rhetoric. And that Brother Ignatius who was once the Cardinal-Minister must be at least as modern as Dostoievsky—or El Greco. The actor's aids to meditation here: "The Grand Inquisitor" and that portrait of the Cardinal of Toledo. The real models, of course, will come to light during the actors' own work—a work that will be most difficult in preparing the role of Sigismund. For despite his resemblances to Caspar Hauser, Prince Myshkin, and the mad Lear, Sigismund must here approach that immediacy against which all our masks of theater and of life protect us. The actor must tear off our prepared faces, must find what *not* to do, must reach the simple impulse or gesture that comes only through the dissolving of our habitual armor. Then, as Grotowski said, he may "fulfil an authentic act" for the spectators. For them and *with* them: so they may find the potential for that act. Finally, what about the Doctor? Given the easy skepticism of our time, we must exercise a prudence that didn't need to concern Hofmannsthal. The script posits a shadowy figure, but he is still too much the Paracelsian sage, the occult reader of signs and souls. We must underplay him. Only as a quiet presence in the background can he become our most adequate witness.

A variety of modes of action, then, within a form of time that is lifting itself out of time. But always a coherent stage-picture. And that means shaping each major tableau as a symbolic confrontation of modes of action within a unifying atmosphere: Olivier and Sigismund; the Doctor and Sigismund; the Doctor and Julian; Basilius and Brother Ignatius; Sigismund and Julian; Sigismund and Basilius . . . and on to the fifth-act meeting of Sigismund and Olivier that will bring us full circle. What provides that unifying atmosphere? *Not* the verbal style of the text. In fact, we'll have to translate the play afresh in order to maintain its lively diversity of idiom. No, we must keep in mind here the address of 1905 that Hofmannsthal delivered to the Shakespeare Society in Weimar—several points of which were reformulated by Buber in 1913 when he wrote "The Space Problem of the Stage" for the Hellerau theater. Shakespeare's characters, Hofmannsthal had said, aren't separated from each other by a "vacuum." They are immersed in a "space mystically alive," a medium that unites them as reciprocal and contrapuntal figures in "a picture of the absolute solitude of the individual" and "of the co-existence of mankind." The face of Portia, he said, is molded from the light that emanates from Brutus. "Or does this light emanate from elsewhere? Are both Brutus and

Portia moulded out of this light and its shadows?" To make visible that atmosphere, that living space constituted by our mutuality, in which whatever occurs between the figures is "filled with a life flowing from the same mysterious sources as the figures themselves," would be to approach the art of Rembrandt.

For Hofmannsthal the crucial ambiguity of Rembrandt is just this: "Who, before a Rembrandt, can say whether the atmosphere is there for the sake of the figures or the figures for the sake of the atmosphere?" That ambiguity, which stresses the *medium* of vision or rendering or living, isn't of merely aesthetic interest. Certain places, Hofmannsthal said, "exist simply to catch the whole light, which is the soul of the atmosphere." Rembrandt's *Night Watch*, we may suppose, is one such place. For Buber the experimental stage at Hellerau would be another: "It is itself something unnamable," he said, "this space. It is shaped by a principle whose name we do not yet know and of which we know only a symbol drawn from the senses: the creative light." And the script of *The Tower* now calls into being another such place—a dark place to catch the whole light. Its updated baroque theatricality, disclosing the one spirit who suffers and acts in apparently solitary figures, seems to have been unlocked by the Faustian key that Hofmannsthal left his Weimar listeners: the merging of "Shakespeare's Atmosphere, Rembrandt's Chiaroscuro, Homer's Myth." Grasping that key, he said, we might descend to the realm of the Mothers and there visualize "the deepest creating and longing of distant spirits in mystical union with the deepest creating and longing of our own epoch—to generate atmosphere for its existence, to let its figures move in the lightness and darkness of life, to imbue its breath with myth."

Words too lofty for us, no doubt, but suggesting the image we must find. The sets? Selective, simplified, architectural. Every shape must be used, must mean. Recall Hofmannsthal's praise for Reinhardt's "analysis of space," his "strong rhythmic faculty," his unique ability "to plan and build up from single elements." Our main impression must be this paradox: a formidable enclosure—but dream-stuff. The tower, the cloisters, the castle rooms—each must be our experienced prisonhouse. And yet this prison is dreamed: the playing areas, seemingly defined by massive architecture, must be enclosed by nothing more solid than light and shadow. Our space must radiate from the stage, too, to include the entire house—for the spectators must perceive a living medium not only between characters but also between the actors and themselves. Though we must use the revolving stage for swift scene-changes, we must sometimes play downstage from our indicated walls and abutments into the arena itself. Reinhardt, as Hofmannsthal said, transformed the actor into "the host of a festival" and the spectator into "an invited guest." We must invite the spectators to find their roles as onlookers *in* our play—so they may find themselves as the locus of our shared dream.

And mustn't they finally apprehend that effect as produced by the light itself? In his essay of 1903, "The Stage as Dream-Image," Hofmannsthal had already proposed that light should become the life-giving force on stage as in dreams. "A single beam which penetrates the night," he said, "may bring into a dream filled with the anxiety of decades of imprisonment such unbearable delight that the dream vanishes and we wake for joy." And he asked: if one such beam can mean salvation to a Gretchen imprisoned by the darkness of the stage, why need anyone build for *Faust* a prison with cardboard prison-bars? But we must go further. Though our theater is neither the Great Hall at Hellerau nor Henri Ronse's tiny Théâtre Oblique, we must let a constantly modulated light *create* the characters—and the whole pattern of our performance must acknowledge that light.

How? Chiaroscuro patterns in each scene: the pseudo-interiors defined by shadow, the light entering through apparent doors or windows. In the first three scenes a deepening evening: before the tower, a room in the tower, and the cloister courtyard—each with its candles and torches illuminating the tableaux. Then the night-scene in the pentagonal tower-room, with the smell of half-burnt straw, where Sigismund drinks the potion and steps into the fiery furnace of our shared dream. Then in Act 3 the queen's death-chamber, darkened, with its eternal lamp—and the daylight sud-denly entering as servants open the wooden shutters of the tall window: the broad daylight of the prophecy, when Sigismund will set his foot on Basilius' neck. Then in Act 4 the castle hall, with the blood-orange of sunset streaming in through the door from the balcony where they watch the executions, deepening to a flaming red when the city burns—all hell broken loose. Finally in Act 5 the antechamber: at first complete darkness, then a kindling of light from flint and steel, then torches, and then the morning sun coming through the window toward which Sig-ismund will step—and reflecting on the wall of his room. Almost as Plato would have it, and just as the stage directions require. Don't Goethe's experiments with stage-lighting and Appia's in-vention of the expressive light-score find their true end in this play that is *about* the sufferings and acts of light?

Study Goethe's color-wheel: the costumes, too, must move with the cycles of light. Sigismund's colors will have to begin with what Goethe called the "passive" or "individual" side of that wheel and move around to the "active" or "universal" as Sigismund moves through passive separation toward unifying action. In the deepening violet of the opening scene, his wolf-skins may seem at first only the bestial counterpart of Olivier's leather-brown. But the Doctor's torch, and the Doctor's own comple-mentary grey-green, will suggest the possibility of transforma-tion. In Act 2, when a Julian in black gives him the potion, Sigismund's fresh cotton suit can be dark blue: a midnight moment of entry into life's dream. In Act 3, Sigismund's courtly attire of fresh green can here confront the hectic purple of Basilius. In Act 4, as the stage directions specify, Sigismund will first appear in a long white shirt with tattered remnants of a scarlet robe: life emerging from death. And in mid-act he can change to a yellow cloak that will be increasingly warmed by the evening sky and the flames of the burning city. Then, in the torchlight and dawn of Act 5, that same cloak can become a gold that plays off against Julian's black and against the leather-and-iron that now completely encloses Olivier. Each tableau, each symbolic confrontation of modes of action, must also be a confrontation of colors: an intense "language of light and darkness," as for the writer of Hofmannsthal's "Letters from a Man Who Returned." It's not a question of mere spectacle. Meditating in 1895 the paintings of the Venetian masters, Hofmannsthal noted "that colors in themselves are nothing but media for the disclosure of the light which passes through them." And he added: "So human beings are also nothing in themselves."

That's just what the actors must come to understand as they try to realize the opposed or complementary objectives they share by analogy: to rule and to serve, to rebel and to submit, to possess and to renounce, to teach and to learn, to read the signs of destiny and to fulfill them, to say the word and to perform the act. We must present the perverse gamut of power that runs from Olivier through Basilius and Julian to Brother Ignatius—masked so often by an equally perverse renunciation. We must show how each prophet or teacher, each reader of destiny—Olivier, Basilius, Julian, Brother Ignatius, the Doctor, Sigismund—can speak only of what he allows to become actual in himself. We must experience through each of these figures the near impossibility of finding an action or suffering that isn't an opacity, a shutting out of the light. Then perhaps—obliquely with Anton, gropingly with the Doctor, in terrifying vulnerability with Sigismund—we may approach that transparent point where the opposed objectives may lose themselves in authoritative service, a shared truth, or a speaking act.

Light itself, as mediated by the colors of our play, becomes the necessary image for that point. Remember Hofmannsthal's comment on the knocking at the gate in *Macbeth*. That scene, he said, is "like the horror-filled end of a dream so powerful that the dream ceases and we awaken"—and it requires of the director all the art, imagination, and strength of soul "with which a great violinist on the brink of some abyss of darkness in Beethoven allows the blooming of pale streaks of mysterious and unreal light." Unreal? Only for those who linger in the dream, deaf or blind to the *music* or the *playing*. Those who

wake, who step with our Sigismund to the window, will know
that such waking is implicit in our action of performance. For
The Tower finally requires of us all what Hofmannsthal said
The Tempest requires of its reader: that we "efface" ourselves,
"become completely empty, become the scene of the action . . . ,
become completely a stage." On this stage, in the action of performance as in the performed action, our emptying in darkness
may be a waking to the whole light. . . .

            First Actor: Am I find-
ing that nameless one who's called Olivier? My objective: to
command. My first word: "Bring fire for my pipe." And my
last: Shoot Sigismund. In this play I'm the beginning and the
end.

  But I pretend not to play. In Act 1, wearing a corporal's
uniform and holding a pike, I stare down the wolf-man. Only
Aron knows me: "You look at men as if they were stones." I
say: "He will command who is chosen by political fate." And
when Julian's servant brings an order, I spit. In Act 2, a cap
over my face, I hear Julian cry "Spirit of light!" and "Son of
fire!" as he gives the cup to the wolf-man who is now called
Sigismund. When they've carried him out and Julian starts to
give me orders, I tell him the job's been done. "Who gave you
permission to act?" "I'm a dragon with many tails," I say. "I
must be used according to my nature." "Must?" But he doesn't
wait for an answer. He'll find it in the hell-fire of Act 4. And
in Act 5, covered with my armor of iron and leather, I'll show
my nature to Sigismund—who will now be fit only to be an
image displayed to the people. "You see that iron thing in my
hand? As my hand grips it and strikes with it, so I myself am
in the hand of fate. What stands before you now is something
you haven't yet known. All you've known up to now is Jesuits'
tricks and hocus-pocus. But what stands here now is reality."
He will turn away. Unusable. We'll have to find a double who
can be shown in his place. And when the Doctor comes in
wringing his hands—"Consider who it is you are going to kill!"
—I will say: "Cut the gestures That priest's and actor's style is
abolished. A sober day has dawned over the world". . . .

*Second
Actor*: And I? Not the mask of the real but the divided soul of
the realist. Hofmannsthal might say that like Ibsen's protagonists I want "to remain in life, but as a secret master, to whom
all others are objects." But doesn't Count Julian act for the
greater glory of God? I have given up the touch of women and
children. I am lonely, find little sleep. I must work in the dark
in order to bring light. That is why in the evening of the first
act I appear on the bridge over the outworks with a soldier and
a lantern—signalling. And why in the night of the last act they
will carry me in and put me on that low bed, surrounded by
rabble with torches, to die. My last word: "Nothing!"

Because
one who tries to bring light into this dark world will find that
he acts on a stage of nothingness. Or so I must tell myself,
despite my early confidence in "God's visible hand." In Act 1,
when I hear the trumpets of the king's messenger, I close my
eyes and see "as through a sudden light" the possibility of a
trial that might place Sigismund on the throne and repay me
for my years of unjust exile. I tell Anton to run with lights for
the messenger. Does it matter that torches are already up along
the stairs? In Act 2 Sigismund drinks from the cup of "flaming
air" so that he may enter "into the light!" "The world depends
upon acts," I say. "Do you know what acts are? Drink and
see." And when they have carried him out, I tell Olivier to
stir up the malcontents and deserters—which he has already
done. There is no time to find out why.

Through all this: a
steely reserve and a secret haste. Every movement tense with
that holding back and racing on. After bringing Sigismund to
Basilius in Act 3, I am in the wings ready to leap into the room,
the royal banner held tight against my body, when Sigismund
fulfills the prophecy by throwing down his father. "Long live
the King!" But because Basilius still lives, I am beaten, stripped
of the royal seal and the chain of my order, and helped only by
that Doctor who reads my soul: "I shall unbar the gates of hell
and make the powers below into my instruments." Then in Act 4

I enter with the servants, disguised and bearing the royal seal, to drive out those who would control Sigismund for darker purposes. We have won: "O my king! My son!—for you come from me who shaped you. . . ." But he doesn't understand. "We are now the prophets and the fulfillers of prophecy," I say. "To perform the acts, that is now our part." And he echoes: "That is our part." But when I point to the flaming sky —"Living proof of my acts"—he fails me, refuses to ride out to help subdue force with force. Why? He simply will not: "But when I say, 'I will,' then you will see how magnificently I go out of this house." Who can wait on such riddling words? Simon reports that Olivier refuses to obey orders. What more can I do? "I have opened the gates of hell, and now all hell is loose. So I must look it in the face."

An excess of light? In Act 5 they carry me in, put me on that bed. Torches. The rabble call themselves "light-bearers" who have been baptized "in the fire." They call Sigismund their light, say that they'll strangle the prince of darkness with their bare hands. But they are blindness itself groping in the dark. "Ha! You nothingness with a thousand heads!" And I will turn away my face from him, too—that creature, that lump of clay to whom I gave the wrong word. Is there a right word? I will close my eyes. "Nothing!" . . .

Third Actor: Neither the real nor the realist, but a potent appearance, a self-conscious image, a name: Basilius. Royalty itself! As Basilius I choose to be nothing but the mask. Behind which—an aching emptiness that watches itself in Richard II's mirror, a void that tries to make castle or cloister into a hall of mirrors within which the king can soliloquize. Doesn't that explain my sudden shifts of tone, my amazingly histrionic sequence of action?

I begin with that set-piece in Act 2—the king standing in the cloister courtyard, playing his own elegiac poet—and run through every powerfully emotional role that my situation might justify. With the Grand Almoner who now calls himself Brother Ignatius, I am at first a shrewd petitioner, then humble, then outraged, and finally the voice of all authority. With Count Julian in the castle, I am the widower who has kept a light burning in my queen's death-chamber, the anxious ruler weighed down by cares of state, the pious father hoping for a worthy son. When I see Sigismund—"The living image of my wife!"—how could I *not* be overcome with tears? I approach him as Saint Martin approached the beggar, grasping my sword only to rend my cloak if he says the word. "Uncover your face!" he pleads. My *face?* "Give me the kiss of peace, my father!" But seeing in his contorted features the desire for power, I become the sly conspirator. "I do not ask you to surrender your teacher to me. I surrender him to you." And when he fails the test, when he turns on me, I am nothing but the terror felt by every powerful image in its moment of truth. But they all rush in, help me to rise. And at once I become firm, decree punishment: the rite of the scaffold, a wholesome spectacle for the people. And how richly I embroider the rite: Zdislaw's son to be imprisoned, the Starosta of Utarkow also to be executed, and Bohuslaw's nieces to be my special jewels for these festive days. In Act 4 am I then outmaneuvered, overcome? Hardly. That confused *coup d'état* allows me to rise to the dignity of the broken image—one who bows with elaborate irony to the Vaivodes who think they have undone me. And when the Chancellor orders the trabants to seize me, I become a little child—yes, that screaming child who has always hidden somewhere behind my eyes and who now hangs onto one leg of the throne, squirming and kicking. Of course, they drag me to my feet, but I leave the stage with a gesture that combines a laudable piety and an ominous strength: "You will witness an edifying miracle if you treat me gently—but whoever shuts me up in a solitary tower will have a desperate man on his hands!" . . .

    Fourth Actor: Nothing behind the histrionic mask but a feverish sensibility that is always watching itself? But there is something else—as he knows who now calls himself Brother Ignatius. Sitting motionless in the cloister courtyard, feeling the brittle weight of his ninety-year-old body, smelling his own stale sweat, hearing the off-stage choir intone Jeremiah's

denunciation of Babylon. Waiting like an actor for his scene
with Basilius to build—each move calculated, and behind each
calculated move an involuntary and silent cry.

That was how
the scene built for us during rehearsal this evening. At first, my
eyes half-closed, just waiting: refusing to see Basilius. Then
saying: "The light of day. A faded gloom. Read out of Guevara."
But opening my eyes before the young monk can raise the book,
and with deliberate eagerness recognizing not Basilius—no,
brushing *him* aside as if he were some buzzing fly—but that
grovelling one-eyed beggar. Then again: "Read from Guevara
as long as it is light." And after the young monk reads, "World
depart from me . . . ," once more brushing aside that buzzing
fly. Then a third time: "Read from Guevara, I am weary that
it is still day." And as the monk reads, Basilius falls on his
knees before me. Now: "I do not know this man!" Laughing
silently. And now, as each of his pleas provokes from me a
more righteously indignant denunciation, letting my voice rise
to a horror that can unlock these words: "But there is something else! You cry out: it is behind your cry and compels you
—ordering you to hear your own cry, to feel your own body,
to bear your body's weight, to watch your body gesture like a
welter of snakes with lashing tails, to breathe your own disso-
lution, to smell your own stink: ear behind ear, nose behind
nose. It despairs behind your despair, horrifies you behind your
horror, and will not let you escape into yourself—because it
knows you and intends to punish you. That is God." Then
sinking back, the secret out—his and mine. And waiting, eyes
closed, for the darkness. . . .

Fifth Actor: Who'd have thought
it? A small part, but count the lines, count the minutes on stage.
A mere servant? No: I watch the play almost from beginning
to end—and may finally understand it. Anton's no fool. If his
shrewdest lines have been cut from the stage version, my gestures still keep their shrewdness. That text of 1925 helps to
give me a subtext. Isn't my triple salute for Olivier just what
he needs? Soldiers deserve all the nose-thumbing compliance
we can give them. With Count Julian, too, it's an easy game:

just play the ironic but faithful servant. He understands—and thinks himself indulgent. The Doctor can be brought around just as quickly: a few shrugs, an aside, and he sees how they're treating Sigismund. And as for that poor beast, I know him as I might know my dog or myself. Gentle enough, but easily frightened or angered. Sometimes quite mad. Julian has taught him to read, and to think like a book. But who's his real teacher and friend? I often make him speak. "Speaking is human," as the 1925 text has me say. "By his speech you know a man." But we don't really need words. The rattle of a pike or just a calm tone of voice: he quiets down, his eyes wide, hands trembling. A child. Maybe that's why it is so rough on me in Act 2 when Julian gives him the cup: I haven't expected anything quite so much like dying.

But then come Acts 3 and 4, with Anton in the midst of things, holding the cups, sending messages, taking in the whole show. After Julian goes out to face hell, who is it in the dawn of Act 5 who strikes a light, listens at the doors, and calls for help? A crucial bit, even if I'm no porter and this isn't *Macbeth*. And after Julian's death, Sigismund says I'll stay with him. From here on it's a strange scene. A naked man with a torch has told him, "Fear not, for *you* are a torch, and no one can extinguish you." Does he believe such stuff? When he talks with Olivier, I prompt him with tactful speeches—but he ignores me. They took away his head at the scaffold, he says. He has stepped behind a wall where he can hear everything but can't be touched. Madness. So when Olivier leaves, I'm ready to act. "Shall we get going? . . . Shall I call somebody? Make signals?" But Sigismund sees the sunlight reflected on the wall and remembers that slaughtered pig he'd spoken of on the night when he took the cup from Julian —remembers how the carcass was hung next to his room, and how the morning sun struck its dark and empty inside. "These are all joyful signs," he says. Joyful! Then we hear voices calling him from the courtyard. I open the window and let in a brighter shaft of light across the room. "I am alone," says Sigismund, as if waking from some dream. He turns toward the window. I warn him to stay back: "They are gesturing like

actors on a stage. They aren't honest people." No use. He calls
them his new friends—and steps into the light.

A shot and the
play's over. Or almost. Only Anton, almost overcome with
anger and grief, tries to keep things moving. Sigismund tells
me to be quiet. The Doctor won't answer me. Then one last
time I make Sigismund speak: "Has our king nothing to say to
us?" He looks at me for a long moment—almost as if he were
back in the cage of Act 1 and I were at the gate, a pike in my
hand. Answering me in the old way, without words. Then he
turns to the Doctor: "Bear witness, I was there, even though no
one knew me." No one? It cuts like death. The Doctor kneels—
we both kneel—and that's it: black-out . . . .

Sixth Actor: "I
was there." As if the "I" that spoke him had already been out-
lived. Or as if our attempt to play what plays among us can
never do more than point to a presence that is already annihilated. Last night I too was there: a Doctor who saw Sigismund
step toward the window, an actor who saw an actor's gesture
for a moment in that clear light.

It's been an awkward business.
Thanks to the cosmological lore that Hofmannsthal has given
the Doctor, my objective has been all too clear: I must point,
through the surrounding darkness, to a field of illumination
whose source remains hidden. The problem has been to justify
my lines, to find some tone that doesn't sound merely portentous.
Even the modesty of this Doctor is embarrassingly rhetorical.
"My fame is a manifold misunderstanding," I say to Julian. "To
those who walk in a mist, every torch looks as big as a church-
door." And I manage a dry laugh. When I have to read Julian's
soul, or Sigismund's—well! The moments of silent observation
have been easier: in Act 4, for instance, when I suddenly understand as I watch Sigismund and Julian look into each other's
eyes why the new king won't ride out to meet force with force.
No doubt that bit prepares for my rather lofty pronouncement
to Olivier in Act 5: "The world will not be ruled by iron, but by
the spirit that is in him." And no doubt it's appropriate that by
then I'm just an ineffectual word-man who gets shoved out of

the way. But by then I'm also one tired actor, drained empty by the effort to maintain something like a necessary tact. So I've been glad to reach the end, when little needs to be said and nothing can be done—except to help catch the falling Sigismund, take him to a chair, feel his pulse, and attend to that swiftly disappearing life.

And last night—after how many times? —that end wasn't just an end. As Sigismund stepped into the shaft of sunlight, something in his gesture—or in my seeing of a gesture that wasn't merely his—made the theater turn inside out. As if the light that always enters our playing-space through windows or from behind walls were really coming from behind the action itself . . . from behind our acting of the action . . . or from behind all seeing of that acting. And suddenly I thought of that place in Act 1 when I say, "Bring a light, I must look him in the eye," and after I've held the torch above his face, he says, "Light is good. . . . Stars are such light. Inside me is a star," and I say, "A beam must have entered him once and awakened the depths." Isn't the abyss of the self always lit from within? As the Doctor must know, Plotinus said it: could we see that sun through the window if the eye weren't sunlike? And Goethe: *Wär nicht das Auge sonnenhaft, / Wie könnten wir das Licht erblicken?* And as the play sped on to somethingg strangely like a fresh beginning, each moment of our attention seemed to share in that light. But if so . . . who bears witness to whom? Light to light? . . .

Seventh Actor: Almost time to strip. To enter the cage, bang the stage with the old horse bone. Relate to those objects. "Wood-lice, worms, toads, devils, vipers! They're all after me." As if you were poor Tom. But don't stop with the objects, with the magic ifs. Hofmannsthal knew that the secret of intense acting, as of the shaman's trance, is to inhabit "two kinds of space at once, that of dreams and that of reality." So enter that dream of accelerated life—and then let the dream break down those "real" walls, undo the lies. "Art is a ripening . . . ," Grotowski says, "which enables us to emerge from darkness into a blaze of light." Yes: from acting into pure action.

For Caspar Hauser a whole education was pressed into four years. And for you now: a couple of hours. Five leaps into the abyss. Each a meeting with what you are, a letting-go of what you thought you were. "Man is a manifold person," says Hofmannsthal, "as he is a manifold pupil." First leap: into the possibility of light. Crouch there in the darkness. Stammering tongue, trembling hands. Hide them. Then the Doctor's firm touch on the sweating forehead: a sudden quiet. "Am I now in the world? Where is the world?" Hauser's questions. The torch then full on the face: "Light is good. . . . Stars are such light." Must you now go back into the dark with your star? (Trakl: *Nachts blieb er mit seinem Stern alein.*) No! Fall to your knees. Stretch out that hand: a human gesture. And hear the Doctor utter Daumer's words, the first words Hauser wrote in his diary: "O man, O man!" (Trakl again: *Gott sprach eine sanfte Flamme zu seinem Herzen. / O Mensch!*) And cry aloud.

Then the second leap: into the fire. Sit there in the half-burnt straw. "My father was in the fire." With a fire-face? "My father has no face!" Now the mother combs your hair, brings back memories: the slaughtered pig, its scream, and yours. Hung up on the cross beam, like that emptied man on the wall. Stretch out your arms. "Mother, where is my end. . . ?" And now Julian, who has taught you everything but can't explain this terrifying word: "Sigismund!" Your fingers run over the cheeks, down the body. "Who is that: I? Where does it have an end?" Hauser's questions. But Julian holds out the cup of flaming air. Must you go back into the dark? No—fall and drink. For his sake, despite his hard words. Then the quiet, the fear going away, the feet growing cold. "Warm them, Anton . . . Lift them into the fiery furnace, where the young men walk singing, my brothers. . . . Face to face! . . . Father—I come—" And the falling.

Then the third leap: into acting . . . as the world knows acting. Brought before your father in a dream: terror. No voice. Down on your knees, face covered. Look up, hear him order you to speak. A whisper comes, then words: 'Uncover your face." "Give me the kiss of peace, my father." But there is no face, no kiss. He tells you to strike Julian. Gives you the ring of power. Now, your first act! That act imagined when you swung the horse bone. And against your teacher? Look hard at this old fox. "Who are you, Satan, who cheats me out of father and mother?" Leap: strike him (your father? yourself?) in the non-face. "I am here now!" Snatch away his sword, force him down, tear off his cloak, put it on. Then throw down the sword. "There! I don't need that! I am the master." And they jump you, bring you down.

And the fourth leap? Into *not* acting. Beyond the scaffold, as in Dostoievsky's letter to his brother: after they've taken your head away. That ripeness. The body ready for speech. Half-carried into the throne-room, installed as king. But your eyes are looking past this spectacle, looking for a friend, for Julian. Who, when he comes, is deaf to your words: walled in. Will you ride out with him in force? "I understand what you want"—your eyes meeting—"but I will not." As when the Beggar's axe in *The Salzburg Great Theatre of the World* drops from his hand—that abstention his one real act. But not here through any miraculous trance: no, in the clearest vision of the real. "I have become ripe, and now I know my place. But it is not where you would have me." How to tell him he dreams? Where does the "I" end? Here and nowhere. "Everything is everywhere," Sacramozo says in *Andreas*, "but only for a moment."

Ready then for the fifth leap: beyond not-acting into action. Beyond this figure of speech called "me." (Sacramozo: "Spirit is action. . . . At some point you are preventing the world from thinking.") So get out of the way. Wake to the play of light. You've told Julian that he will see how magnificently you go out of this house. Now watch them bring him in from the fire, dying, put him on that bed. When he rages at these naked ones, these baptized in the fire, step toward him: "For what is worth the trouble of saying, the tongue is too thick." When he turns his blind hate upon you, step nearer: "My teacher, I am with you." Give back the word he put under your tongue—the word of comfort in the solitude of this life:

face to face, as you drink now from the vein he opened within you but will not see. (Sacramozo: "Attention means as much as love. . . . Who is attentive?") And when these naked ones call, speak to them as to yourself: "Yes, I will go out with you." Into the open field. But not yet. You must face that nameless one who, four acts ago, stared down a cringing wolfman. Now answer his taunts—in words, in silence. You are here and not here. He can't see you: "your eyes are walled up with what is not." Speak the truth: "Such as you, I have always had sitting around me in my pigsty." Such as you. Then, prodigal, turn your back on that familiar shadow, walk out of this sty—to return, in a moment, as morning breaks. On the wall, a faint light: like that which might strike the carcass of a slaughtered pig. Through the window, voices calling. Will you go forward and never look back? Into the open—where players are no longer separate from the play? "I am alone and long to be united." Rising now, turning toward the window, the new friends. ("You know who I am," Hauser says to the Sun. "My eyes want to see you always.") And now letting all the words, the gestures, drop: simply to step . . . shot through. . . .

Houselights are going down. Time to strip. Get in the cage. Bang the stage with the horse bone. Let this nameless one come to the dark tower. . . .

And as the houselights dim, rousing us from the daydream or chatter in which we have been immersed, we discover a blue-violet evening sky: a background of active light that sculpts the outworks in jagged relief and then loses itself in the darkness of a small open cage at the tower's base. From that point at stage left, the architectural motifs of closure expand in irregular rhythm: back through the angled blocks of the outworks to the now perceptibly fading sky, laterally and forward across the arena to the triply banked seats where we wait. In the shadow of the walls, a group of soldiers. At the rear of the cage, an erratic banging. A corporal calls for fire to light his pipe. A recruit brings a glowing brand, holds it up: a smoking red-orange that makes the shadows leap back-

ward and almost annihilates in our vision the last hint of the sky's blue-violet. Eyes glint in the corporal's face—and in the face of someone crouched at the rear of the cage, whose banging becomes more frenzied. Grasping an iron pike, the corporal stalks with some bravado toward the gate of the cage. Witnesses, implicit actors, we wake to the play: . . .

SOME TEXTS BEHIND
THE TEXT

I LIST here the fairly modern texts that bear most importantly on this essay: scripts, sources of background information, critical works that have been especially illuminating or provocative, and a few of the speculative works that have helped to shape my horizon in all weathers. Asterisks identify the scripts or translations that have been followed in the detailed commentaries.

Certain texts have radically affected my course of thought or have quite often intersected it:

Bentley, Eric. *The Playwright as Thinker*. Rev. ed. New York, 1955.
———. *Theatre of War*. New York, 1973.
Brook, Peter. *The Empty Space*. New York, 1968.
Brustein, Robert. *The Theatre of Revolt*. Boston, 1968.
Buber, Martin. *Between Man and Man*. Tr., Ronald Gregor Smith. London, 1947.
———. *Daniel: Dialogues on Realization*. Tr., Maurice Friedman. New York, 1964.
———. *I and Thou*. Tr., Ronald Gregor Smith. 2nd ed. New York, 1958.
———. *The Knowledge of Man*. Ed., Maurice Friedman. New York, 1965.
———. *Martin Buber and the Theater*. Ed., Maurice Friedman. New York, 1970.
———. *Pointing the Way*. Ed., Maurice Friedman. New York, 1963.
Coomaraswamy, Ananda K. *Am I My Brother's Keeper?* New York, 1947.
———. *The Transformation of Nature in Art*. 2nd ed. Cambridge, Mass., 1934.
Fergusson, Francis. *The Idea of a Theater*. Princeton, 1949.
Ghose, Aurobindo. *Essays on the Gita*. New York, 1950.
Lavelle, Louis. *De l'Acte*. Paris, 1937.
———. *La Parole et l'écriture*. Paris, 1942.

Lavelle, Louis. *La Presence totale*. Paris, 1934.

Marcel, Gabriel. *Being and Having: An Existentialist Diary*. Intro., James Collins. New York, 1965.

————. *Creative Fidelity*. Tr., Robert Rosthal. New York, 1964.

Styan, J. L. *The Elements of Drama*. Cambridge, 1960.

Other texts are behind only one or two chapters:

1: SPEAKING OF PLAYING

Borges, Jorge Luis. *Labyrinths*. Ed., Donald A. Yates and James E. Irby. New York, 1964.

————. *Other Inquisitions 1937–1952*. Tr., Ruth L. C. Simms. New York, 1965.

Cervantes Saavedra, Miguel de. *Don Quixote of La Mancha*. Tr., Walter Starkie. New York, 1964.

Hecht, Werner. "The Development of Brecht's Theory of Epic Theatre, 1918–1933." *Tulane Drama Review*, 6 (Autumn, 1961), 40–97.

Hofmannsthal, Hugo von. "A Prologue to Brecht's *Baal*." Tr., Alfred Schwarz. *Tulane Drama Review*, 6 (Autumn, 1961), 111–122.

————. *Selected Plays and Libretti*. Ed., Michael Hamburger. New York, 1963.

"Hofmannsthal und Buber: Briefe, 1926–28." *Neue Rundschau*, 73 (1962), 757–761.

Merleau-Ponty, Maurice. *Signs*. Tr., Richard C. McCleary. Evanston, 1964.

Polanyi, Michael. *Personal Knowledge: Towards a Post-Critical Philosophy*. Chicago, 1958.

Rilke, Rainer Maria. *The Notebooks of Malte Laurids Brigge*. Tr., M. D. Herter Norton. New York, 1949.

Schiller, Friedrich. *On the Aesthetic Education of Man*. Tr., Reginald Snell. London, 1954.

2: PLAYING THE PLAYER

(*Note*: I do not list here a number of scripts that are given brief mention in this chapter.)

Abel, Lionel. *Metatheatre*. New York, 1963.

Beckett, Samuel. *Endgame*. New York, 1958.

*————. *Happy Days*. New York, 1961.

*————. *Oh les beaux jours*. Paris, 1963.

Brecht, Bertolt. "Studium des ersten Auftritts Shakespeares 'Coriolan.' " In *Gesammelte Werke*. Frankfurt am Main, 1967. Vol. XVI. Pp. 869–888.
Cohn, Ruby. *Samuel Beckett: The Comic Gamut*. New Brunswick, N.J., 1962.
Coleman, D. C. "Fun and Games: Two Pictures of Heartbreak House." *Drama Survey*, 5 (Winter, 1966–67), 223–236.
Driver, Tom F. *Romantic Quest and Modern Query: A History of the Modern Theatre*. New York, 1970.
Esslin, Martin. *Brecht: The Man and his work*. Rev. ed. New York, 1971.
Genet, Jean. *The Balcony*. Rev. ed. Tr., Bernard Frechtman. New York, 1966.
Kott, Jan. *Theatre Notebook: 1947–1967*. Tr., Boleslaw Taborski. New York, 1968.
Schechner, Richard. *Environmental Theater*. New York, 1973.
*Stoppard, Tom. *Rosencrantz & Guildenstern Are Dead*. New York, 1967.

3: KILLING OURSELVES

Bradbrook, M. C. *Ibsen the Norwegian*. London, 1948.
Downs, Brian. *Ibsen: The Intellectual Background*. London, 1946.
Freud, Sigmund. "Some Character-Types Met with in Psychoanalytic Work." In James W. McFarlane, ed., *Henrik Ibsen: A Critical Anthology*. London, 1970. Pp. 392–399.
Hofmannsthal, Hugo von. *Selected Prose*. Trs., Mary Hottinger and Tania and James Stern. New York, 1952.
————. "The People in Ibsen's Dramas." In James W. McFarlane, ed., *Discussions of Henrik Ibsen*. Boston, 1962. Pp. 83–88.
Ibsen, Henrik. *Brand*. Tr., Michael Meyer, with intro. by W. H. Auden. New York, 1960.
*————. *Ghosts and Three Other Plays*. Tr., Michael Meyer. New York, 1966.
*————. *Hedda Gabler and Three Other Plays*. Tr., Michael Meyer. New York, 1961.
————. *The Oxford Ibsen*. Tr. and ed., James W. McFarlane. London, 1960–72.
————. *Peer Gynt*. Tr., Rolf Fjelde. New York, 1964.
*————. *When We Dead Awaken and Three Other Plays*. Tr., Michael Meyer. New York, 1960.
Koht, Halfdan. *The Life of Ibsen*. New York, 1931.

Maeterlinck, Maurice. *The Treasure of the Humble.* Tr., Alfred Sutro. London, 1907.

Mallarmé, Stéphane. "Hamlet and Fortinbras." In *Mallarmé: Selected Prose Poems, Essays, and Letters.* Tr., Bradford Cook. Baltimore, 1956.

Maritain, Jacques. *The Dream of Descartes.* Tr., Mabelle L. Andison. New York, 1944.

Meyer, Michael. *Ibsen: A Biography.* New York, 1971.

Northam, John. *Dividing Worlds.* New York, 1965.

Sartre, Jean-Paul. *Being and Nothingness.* Tr., Hazel E. Barnes. New York, 1956.

Shaw, Bernard. *The Quintessence of Ibsenism.* In *The Works of Bernard Shaw.* Standard Edition. Vol. 19. London, 1932.

Strindberg, August. "Psychic Murder (Apropos *Rosmersholm*)." *The Drama Review,* 13 (Winter, 1968), 113–118.

Valency, Maurice. *The Flower and the Castle.* New York, 1963.

Weigand, Hermann J. *The Modern Ibsen.* New York, 1925.

4: SEEING THE HIDDEN

Artaud, Antonin. "Production Plan for Strindberg's *Ghost Sonata.*" *Tulane Drama Review,* 8 (Winter, 1963), 50–57.

Corrigan, Robert. "Strindberg and the Abyss." In August Strindberg, *A Dream Play and The Ghost Sonata.* Tr., C. R. Mueller. San Francisco, 1966.

Herbert, Jean. Ed. *Études sur Ramana Maharshi.* Paris, 1972.

Humphreys, Christmas. Ed. *The Wisdom of Buddhism.* New York, 1961.

Lamm, Martin. *August Strindberg.* Tr., Harry G. Carlson. New York, 1971.

Lunin, Hanno. *Strindbergs Dramen.* Emsdetten, 1962.

Northam, John. "Strindberg's *Spook Sonata.*" In Carl Smedmark, ed., *Essays on Strindberg.* Stockholm, 1966. Pp. 39–48.

Rilke, Rainer Maria. *Wartime Letters of Rainer Maria Rilke, 1914–1921.* Tr., M. D. Herter Norton. New York, 1940.

Ronse, Henri. "Pour un théâtre oblique." *Obliques* I (1972), 87–92.

Schopenhauer, Arthur. *The World as Will and Idea.* Tr., R. B. Haldane and J. Kemp. 4th ed. London, 1896.

Strindberg, August. *The Chamber Plays.* Trs., Evert Sprinchorn, Seabury Quinn, Jr., and Kenneth Petersen. New York, 1962.

———. *Open Letters to the Intimate Theater.* Ed., Walter Johnson. Seattle, 1966.

*————. *The Plays of Strindberg.* Tr., Michael Meyer. Vol. 1. New York, 1964.

————. *Schwarze Fahnen.* Tr., Emil Schering. München, 1920.

————. *Zones of the Spirit.* Tr., Claud Field. London, 1913.

Swerling, Anthony. *Strindberg's Impact in France, 1920–1960.* Cambridge, 1971.

Törnquist, Egil. "Ingmar Bergman Directs Strindberg's *Ghost Sonata.*" *Theatre Quarterly,* 3 (Jul.–Sept. 1973), 3–14.

Valency, Maurice. *The Flower and the Castle.* New York, 1963.

Vowles, Richard B. "Strindberg's *Isle of the Dead.*" *Modern Drama,* 5 (1962), 366–378.

Wei Wu Wei. *The Tenth Man.* Hong Kong, 1971.

World Theater, 11 (1962), Special Strindberg Number.

5: Dreaming the Music

Barrault, Jean-Louis. *The Theatre of Jean-Louis Barrault.* Tr., Joseph Chiari. New York, 1961.

Beaumont, Ernest. *The Theme of Beatrice in the Plays of Claudel.* London, 1954.

Bentley, Eric. *Bernard Shaw: 1856–1950.* New York, 1957.

Berst, Charles A. *Bernard Shaw and the Art of Drama.* Urbana, 1973.

Butor, Michel. *La Modification.* Paris, 1957.

Chekhov, Anton. *The Oxford Chekhov.* Ed., Ronald Hingley. Vol. 3. London, 1964.

*————. *Six Plays.* Tr., Robert Corrigan. New York 1962.

*Claudel, Paul. *Break of Noon.* Tr., Wallace Fowlie. Chicago, 1960.

————. *Correspondance Paul Claudel/Jean-Louis Barrault.* Ed., Michel Lioure. Cahiers Paul Claudel, 10. Paris, 1974.

————. *Journal.* Paris, 1968–69.

————. *Mémoires improvisés.* Paris, 1969.

————. *Mes Idées sur le théâtre.* Paris, 1966.

————. *Oeuvres complètes.* Paris, 1950–74.

————. *Théâtre.* Rev. ed. Paris, 1967–71.

Clurman, Harold. "Notes for a Production of *Heartbreak House.*" In *On Directing.* New York, 1972. Pp. 229–241.

Dukore, Bernard. *Bernard Shaw, Playwright.* Columbia, Mo., 1973.

Farabet, René. *Le Jeu de l'acteur dans le théâtre de Claudel.* Paris, 1960.

Gerhardi, William. *Anton Chekhov: A Critical Study.* London, 1923.

Howells, Bernard. "The Enigma of *Partage de Midi*: A Study in Ambiguity." In Richard Griffiths, ed., *Claudel: A Reappraisal*. London, 1968. Pp. 19–33.

Kitchin, Laurence. *Mid-Century Drama*. 2nd ed. London, 1962.

Knowles, Dorothy. *French Drama of the Inter-War Years*. London, 1967.

Leary, Daniel. "Shaw's Use of Stylized Characters and Speech in *Man and Superman*." *Modern Drama*, 5 (1963), 477–490.

Lioure, Michel. *L'Esthétique dramatique de Paul Claudel*. Paris, 1971.

Lucas, F. L. *The Drama of Chekhov, Synge, Yeats, and Pirandello*. London, 1963.

McDowell, Frederick P. W. "Technique, Symbol, and Theme in *Heartbreak House*." *PMLA*, 68 (1953), 335–356.

Madaule, Jacques. *Le Drame de Paul Claudel*. Rev. ed. Paris, 1964.

Magarshack, David. *Chekhov, the Dramatist*. London, 1952.

Meisel, Martin. *Shaw and the Nineteenth-Century Theatre*. Princeton, 1969.

Plourde, Michel. *Paul Claudel: Une Musique du silence*. Montréal, 1970.

*Shaw, Bernard. *The Works of Bernard Shaw*. Standard Edition. London, 1930–34.

Simmons, Ernest J. *Chekhov: A Biography*. Boston, 1962.

Stanislavsky, Constantin. *Building a Character*. Tr., E. R. Hapgood. New York, 1948.

———. *My Life in Art*. Tr., J. J. Robbins. Boston, 1925.

States, Bert O. *Irony and Drama: A Poetics*. Ithaca, 1971.

Stroeva, M. N. "*The Three Sisters* in the Production of the Moscow Art Theater." In Robert Louis Jackson, ed., *Chekhov: A Collection of Critical Essays*. Englewood Cliffs, N.J., 1967. Pp. 121–135.

Styan, J. L. *Chekhov in Performance*. Cambridge, 1971.

Valency, Maurice. *The Breaking String*. New York, 1966.

———. *The Cart and the Trumpet*. New York, 1973.

Watson, Harold. *Claudel's Immortal Heroes: A Choice of Deaths*. New Brunswick, N.J., 1971.

Weintraub, Stanley. *Journey to Heartbreak*. New York, 1971.

Wisenthal, J. L. *The Marriage of Contraries: Bernard Shaw's Middle Plays*. Cambridge, Mass. 1974.

6. UNDOING

Beckett, Samuel. *En attendant Godot.* Paris, 1952.

*————. *Endgame.* New York, 1958.

————. *Fin de partie.* Paris, 1957.

————. *Waiting for Godot.* New York, 1954.

Benoit, Hubert. *The Supreme Doctrine.* New York, 1959.

Bentley, Eric. *The Life of the Drama.* New York, 1964.

Berne, Eric. *Games People Play.* New York, 1964.

Burke, Kenneth. "Antony in Behalf of the Play." In *The Philosophy of Literary Form.* 2nd ed. Baton Rouge, 1967. Pp. 329–343.

Cavell, Stanley. "Ending the Waiting Game." In *Must We Mean What We Say?* New York, 1969. Pp. 115–162.

Coe, Richard. *The Vision of Jean Genet.* New York, 1968

Cohn, Ruby. *Samuel Beckett: The Comic Gamut.* New Brunswick, N.J., 1962.

Copeau, Jacques. *Notes sur le métier de comédien.* Paris, 1955.

————. *Registres I: Appels.* Eds., Marie-Hélène Dasté and Suzanne Maistre Saint-Denis. Paris, 1974.

Doisy, Marcel. *Jacques Copeau: ou l'absolut dans l'art.* Paris, 1954.

Driver, Tom. *Romantic Quest and Modern Query: A History of the Modern Theatre.* New York, 1970.

Esslin, Martin. *The Theatre of the Absurd.* Rev. ed. New York, 1969.

Genet, Jean. *Le Balcon.* Paris, 1956.

————. *The Balcony.* Tr., Bernard Frechtman. New York, 1960.

*————. *The Balcony.* Tr., Bernard Frechtman. New York, 1966.

————. *Oeuvres complètes.* Paris, 1967–68.

————. *Our Lady of the Flowers.* Tr., Bernard Frechtman. New York, 1964.

Goldman, Michael. *The Actor's Freedom: Toward a Theory of Drama.* New York, 1975.

Grossvogel, David. *The Blasphemers.* Ithaca, 1965.

Hoffman, Frederick J. *Samuel Beckett: The Language of Self.* New York, 1963.

Ionesco, Eugene. *Notes and Counter Notes.* Tr., Donald Watson. New York, 1964.

Jacobsen, Josephine, and William R. Mueller. *Ionesco and Genet: Playwrights of Silence.* New York, 1968.

Kenner, Hugh. *Samuel Beckett.* 2nd ed. New York, 1968

Kurtz, Maurice. *Jacques Copeau, biographie d'un théâtre.* Paris, 1950.

MacClintock, Landor. *The Age of Pirandello.* Bloomington, 1951.

Nelson, Benjamin. "*The Balcony* and Parisian Existentialism." *Tulane Drama Review,* 7 (Spring, 1963), 60–79.

Nelson, Robert J. *Play within a Play.* New Haven, 1958.

Pirandello, Luigi. *Maschere Nude.* Milano, 1950.

*————. *Naked Masks.* Ed., Eric Bentley. New York, 1952.

Robbe-Grillet, Alain. "Samuel Beckett, or 'Presence' in the Theatre." In Martin Esslin, ed., *Samuel Beckett: A Collection of Critical Essays.* Englewood Cliffs, N.J., 1965. Pp. 108–116.

Sartre, Jean-Paul. *Saint Genet: Actor and Martyr.* New York, 1964.

Styan, J. L. *The Dark Comedy.* Rev. ed. Cambridge, 1967.

Suzuki, D. T., Erich Fromm, and Richard De Martino. *Zen Buddhism and Psychoanalysis.* New York, 1963.

Thody, Philip. *Jean Genet.* New York, 1969.

Unamuno, Miguel de. *The Tragic Sense of Life.* Tr., J. E. Crawford Flitch. New York, 1954.

Vittorini, Domenico. *The Drama of Luigi Pirandello.* London, 1935.

Weales, Gerald. "The Language of *Endgame.*" *Tulane Drama Review,* 6 (Summer, 1962), 107–117.

7: BEARING WITNESS

Artaud, Antonin. *The Theater and Its Double.* Tr., M. C. Richards. New York, 1958.

Berliner Ensemble, eds. *Theaterarbeit.* Dresden, 1952.

Brecht, Bertolt. *Brecht on Theatre.* Tr., John Willett. New York, 1966.

*————. *Collected Plays.* Ed., Ralph Manheim and John Willett. Vol. 7. New York, 1975.

————. *Gesammelte Werke.* Frankfurt am Main, 1967.

————. *The Messingkauf Dialogues.* Tr., John Willett. London, 1965.

Browne, E. Martin. *The Making of T. S. Eliot's Plays.* Cambridge, 1969.

Burckhardt, Carl J. *Erinnerung an Hofmannsthal.* München, 1964.

Coghlan, Brian. *Hofmannsthal's Festival Dramas.* Cambridge, 1964.

Eliot, T. S. *Collected Poems, 1909–1962.* New York, 1963.

————. *The Complete Plays.* New York, 1969.

*————. *Murder in the Cathedral.* New York, 1963.

————. *Selected Essays.* 2nd ed. New York, 1950.

Esslin, Martin. *Brecht: The Man and his Work.* Rev. ed. New York, 1971.

Fuegi, John. *The Essential Brecht.* Los Angeles, 1972.

Ghéon, Henri. *The Art of the Theatre.* Tr., Adele M. Fiske. New York, 1961.

Goethe, Johann W. von. *Goethes Farbenlehre.* Ed., Rupprecht Matthaei. Ravensburg, 1971.

Gray, Ronald. *Brecht the Dramatist.* Cambridge, 1976.

Grotowski, Jerzy. *Towards a Poor Theatre.* Ed., Eugenio Barba. London, 1969.

Hecht, Werner. *Materialen zu Brechts "Der Kaukasische Kreidekreis."* Frankfurt am Main, 1966.

Hederer, Edgar. *Hugo von Hofmannsthal.* Frankfurt am Main, 1960.

Hennenberg, Fritz. *Dessau-Brecht Musikalische Arbeiten.* Berlin, 1963.

*Hofmannsthal, Hugo von. *Gesammelte Werke in Einzelausgaben.* Frankfurt am Main, 1945–59

————. "The People in Ibsen's Dramas." In James W. McFarlane, ed., *Discussions of Henrik Ibsen.* Boston, 1962. Pp. 83–88.

————. "A Prologue to Brecht's Baal." Tr., Alfred Schwarz. *Tulane Drama Review,* 6 (Autumn, 1961), 111–122.

————. *Selected Plays and Libretti.* Ed., Michael Hamburger. New York, 1963.

————. *Selected Prose.* Trs., Mary Hottinger and Tania and James Stern. New York, 1952.

————. *Three Plays.* Tr., Alfred Schwarz. Detroit, 1966.

————. "Vienna Letter." *Dial,* 74 (1923), 281–288.

"Hofmannsthal und Buber: Briefe, 1926–28." *Neue Rundschau,* 73 (1962), 757–761.

Howarth, Herbert. *Notes on Some Figures Behind T. S. Eliot.* Boston, 1964.

Hurwicz, Angelika. *Brecht Inszeniert: Der Kaukasische Kreidekreis.* Velber bei Hannover, 1964.

Jones, David E. *The Plays of T. S Eliot.* London, 1960.

Kenner, Hugh. *The Invisible Poet.* New York, 1959.

Maccoby, H. Z. "Thomas's Temptation." In David B Clark, ed., *Twentieth-Century Interpretations of "Murder in the Cathedral."* Englewood Cliffs, N.J., 1971. Pp. 93–96.

Martz, Louis. "The Saint as Tragic Hero: *Saint Joan* and *Murder in the Cathedral.*" In Cleanth Brooks, ed., *Tragic Themes in Western Literature.* New Haven, 1955. Pp. 150–178.

Nagler, A. M. "Hugo von Hofmannsthal and Theater." *Theatre Research,* 2 (1960), 5–15.

Politzer, Heinz. "How Epic is Bertolt Brecht's Epic Theatre?" In Travis Bogard and William I. Oliver, eds., *Modern Drama: Essays in Criticism.* New York, 1965. Pp. 54–72.

Ronse, Henri. "Pour un théâtre oblique." *Obliques* I (1972), 87–92.

Sayler, Oliver M. Ed. *Max Reinhardt and His Theatre.* New York, 1924.

Schwartz, Egon. "Hofmannsthal and the Problem of Reality." *Wisconsin Studies in Contemporary Literature,* 8 (1967), 484–504.

Simonson, Lee. *The Stage is Set.* New York, 1932.

Smith, Carol. *T. S. Eliot's Dramatic Theory and Practice.* Princeton, 1963.

Smith, Grover C., Jr. *T. S. Eliot's Poetry and Plays.* Chicago, 1956.

Spanos, William V. *The Christian Tradition in Modern Verse Drama.* New Brunswick, N.J., 1967.

Speaight, Robert. "Interpreting Becket and Other Parts." In Neville Braybrooke, ed., *T. S. Eliot: A Symposium.* New York, 1958. Pp. 70–78.

Trakl, Georg. *Selected Poems.* Ed., Christopher Middleton. London, 1968.

Wassermann, Jacob. *Caspar Hauser.* Tr., Caroline Newton. New York, 1928.

Weales, Gerald. *Religion in Modern English Drama.* Philadelphia, 1961.

Wittmann, Lothar. *Sprachthematik und dramatische Form im Werke Hofmannsthals.* Stuttgart, 1966.

INDEX

LIBRARY OF CONGRESS CATALOGING IN PUBLICATION DATA

Whitaker, Thomas R.
 Fields of play in modern drama.

 Includes index.
  1. Drama—19th century—History and criticism.
 2. Drama—20th century—History and criticism.
 I. Title.
 PN1851.W45   809.2   76-45916
 ISBN 0-691-06333-8